50 Principles of Composition in Photography

A practical guide to
seeing photographically through
the eyes of a master photographer

by Klaus Bohn, MPA, F/SPPA, A
www.photographicartvictoria.com

CCB Publishing
British Columbia, Canada

50 Principles of Composition in Photography: A practical guide to seeing photographically through the eyes of a master photographer

Copyright ©2006 by Klaus Bohn, MPA, F/SPPA, A
ISBN-10   0-9739050-9-3
ISBN-13   978-0-9739050-9-0
First Edition

Library and Archives Canada Cataloguing in Publication

Bohn, Klaus, 1945-
50 principles of composition in photography : a practical guide to seeing photographically through the eyes of a master photographer / by Klaus Bohn.
Includes index.
Also available in electronic format.
ISBN 0-9739050-9-3
1. Composition (Photography). I. Title. II. Title: Fifty principles of composition in photography.
TR146.B65 2006   771   C2006-903068-5

Photo credits: All photos contained herein are copyright Klaus Bohn with the following exceptions:
1)   Page 92: Mitch Hippsley
2)   Pages 64, 84: David Bohn
3)   Pages 56, 96: Paul Rabinovitch

Publisher: CCB Publishing
                 British Columbia, Canada
                 www.ccbpublishing.com

Dedication

I dedicate this book to my three children who, even at an early age, have spurred me on to live a life full of adventure with them. I'm glad that my adventure, my pursuit for daily living is so much more than just making a living! That is borne out even in their lives as they have grown into adulthood.

To you Michael, my first born, I dedicate this book because you were there when I needed you the most. Tests and trials are inevitable but as we face each challenge, what enables us to weather the storm is those who are there for us and are willing to go the extra mile. They give up their own comfort for another and stick with their commitment to help another. Words cannot express my gratitude to you my son. You helped me start over and stayed five years with me.

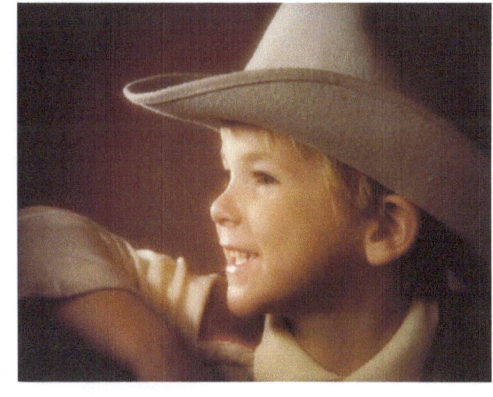

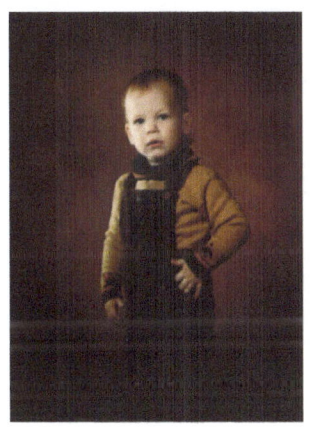

To you David who bears my name David Klaus, or DK for short, you were so adventuresome when after high school you left home and pioneered for a place in Victoria, British Columbia. In time we followed and moved too. I could tell at an early age that you had an eye and ear for art and music in just how you dedicated your time and efforts and from your many accomplishments. Without your help and sheer determination to put it all together this book would never have happened. During the past five years we have learned from each other, your commercial approach and my portrait method combined to help us find our individual style. For this I thank you from the bottom of my heart.

To Tammy my only daughter, who echoes my personality in so many ways, especially in travel. As you know I put a lot of effort into travelling to many far away places and now you too have shone so much brightness in your many travels to so many far away places. I highly regard your invitation to travel with you to the Orient and other places that can be shared so personally with family as I have valued in the past. When you were small I very often used you as a model. You will always remember one special project which was an adventure in itself. I had one year to photograph you each month with a different animal: a pig, a lamb, a cat, a horse, a cow, a dog and so on. Thank you for being you.

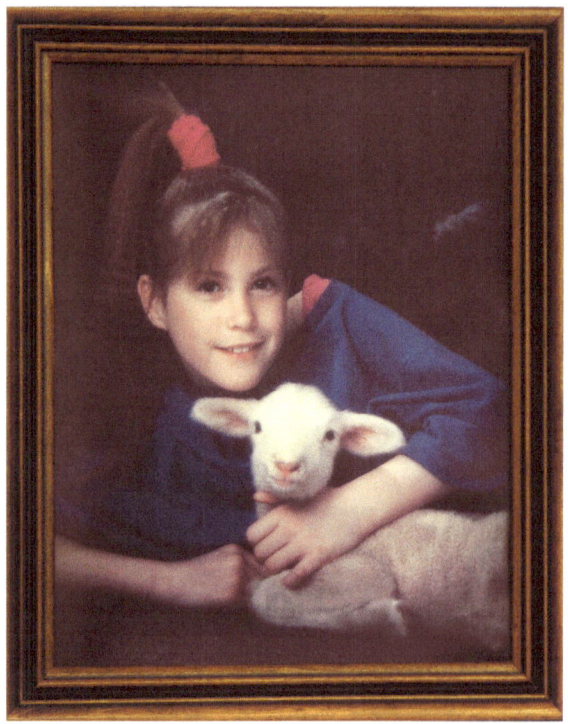

Table of Contents

Foreword

Picture yourself alone in a car driving down the highway. To the right is a large body of water, to the left are hills and telephone poles, in front is a car coming towards you and in back is nothing. You have been over the same stretch of road on numerous occasions, but this time something is different. The trip seems more relaxing and far more interesting. Let's take a second look!

It is the first day of summer. The radio is resounding a soothing tune. The sun is beating its hot rays down onto the lake. As they hit the water, the rays seem to bounce as though dancing from wave to wave, twinkling as they step. Ducks sit calmly while the waves carry them ever so gently through the flowing water.

The car ahead is travelling in a mirage as the heat rises from the pavement. The highway over which you have just journeyed awaits the next vehicle. What will the travellers inside see out their windows?

No wonder the trip seems so much more interesting! My eyes have been opened to a new dimension, one which was always there, but which I was taking for granted and not seeing. We get so involved in our day to day living and the hustle and bustle that goes with it, that we are missing much of the beauty around us.

Klaus' book, *50 Principles of Composition in Photography*, is one that I feel will help you, whether you are amateur or professional photographers. Each of us has something to learn about viewing our surroundings and how best to capture the feeling and emotion that goes along with the view. The book is basic enough for all to read and understand. Even if just one principle is gained by studying the pages, you have been enriched.

Take a moment now to look around you. What do you see? There is likely a lot more there than you realize. There are lots of photographs waiting to be taken. There are lots of photographs waiting to be taken right where you are this moment.

Open your eyes! Read on!

Judith Barber
Professor of Business Studies

Introduction

According to Webster's definition, "composition" is a "putting together of a whole, the make-up of anything and/or a mixture of substance."

There are **no rules to composition**, only guides and extremely flexible principles that may help us to see more sensitively instead of in a hit or miss manner. The more aware we are of effective composition, the more satisfaction we may derive from photography. Learning to give form and balance by putting together the elements harmoniously can help us see a subject in the strongest way.

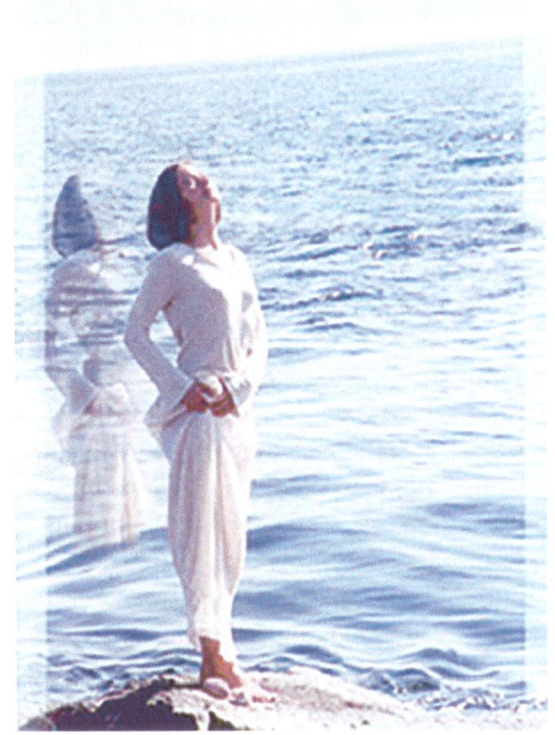

Learning the ABC's of photography begins with the technical education of our equipment and light. Composition is an elementary step. Most beginners are in search of a formula or recipe to which they can rigidly adhere. This, of course, is an illusion! Any recipe for good composition is similar to that of a chef who begins to work instinctively -- a dash of this and a pinch of that. We must remember that composition is the selection and arrangement of an object within the picture format by using space most effectively.

Photography, being communicative, means we must learn to compose our meaning using the least number of elements to tell the story in the briefest way. Showing as much as we need, but no more! The basic decision is thus, "What to include, and what to leave out." *Brevity is the economy of means.*

Photography brings a visual language that is universal in understanding. We must then understand its vocabulary which consists of shapes, textures, patterns, lines, colours, shade of light to dark and sharp to blurry images. Just as we must learn to arrange words in a coherent order in order to make sense when we write or speak, so too must we put visual elements together in an organized manner if our photographs are to convey their meaning clearly and vividly.

Composition means arrangement: the orderly putting together of parts to make a unified whole; composition through a personal, intuitive act. However, there are basic principles that govern the way visual elements behave and interact when you combine them inside the four borders of a photograph. Once we have sharpened our vision and grasped these basic ideas of principles, then we will have the potential for making our photographs more exciting and effective than ever before.

Photographers live through their eyes. The basic way of photographic "seeing" is an essential step in being able to communicate photographically. In mastering composition, one must cultivate the ability to see shapes, lines, forms, masses, etc., and not to just recognize objects. Even more importantly than that, we must be able to visualize in our mind's eye just how the objects will look when they are reproduced on a flat piece of paper. This is brought out only through practice and experience. Through practice, this procedure should become second nature; an unconscious, automatic habit. By knowing the format of a photograph, we can then learn to pre-visualize the photograph in a positive and effective manner. Remember, seeing involves the mind as well as the eyes.

Painters have total freedom when it comes to putting what they want into their painting. Photographers are restricted to recording what is in front of their lens. The space fenced off by the four edges of the camera's ground glass is the photographic area. The photographer has an advantage over the painter, though, in being able to freeze a split second of time -- peak action. By using space effectively and not just filling it, the arranging of shapes and tones within the area can help convey the photograph's meaning and help reinforce its emotional effect. But what should be included or excluded? How big should you make things? Where should you place an object in relation to another object, and in relation to the edges of the photograph? These principles will be discussed in full.

By what criteria or standard do we judge a photograph as good or bad? The eye and mind expect certain things in order to enjoy certain things. If the photograph fulfills these expectations then it is basically a success. One of the simple tricks of composition is to keep the eye from running out of the picture before it has been fully satisfied. When watching for this, there are **three essential qualifications**:

1. **Good technical quality (focus, light, exposure, etc.)**
2. **Interest or impact (storytelling)**
3. **Good composition (keeps the eye in the photograph)**

As mentioned, there are no ironclad rules that we must follow for composition, just principles or guides for ease of expression i.e. something that can be understood universally with a historical continuum in influencing the photograph being composed.

The fifty principles of composition presented in this book will greatly benefit both amateur and professional photographers in developing their own photographic art.

This work is meant as a guide or learning tool, versus an art or coffee table book. With this in mind all photographers, whether they be artists or craftsmen, may appreciate the images chosen to demonstrate these fifty principles of composition in photography.

Photography: Unlike the Other "Fine" Arts

Painting, sculpture and many other fine arts are performed by dexterity coupled with talent, which is the ability to see and perceive the harmony of parts not necessarily in front of the artist.

Photography cannot be performed without the subject being in front of the lens. Consequently, it is a reproduction type of art. Not belittling the ability to manipulate the machinery and, of course, the talent to see and put together the photograph using composition in an appealing manner. To be an elite photographer, it goes without saying that one must know their equipment completely, performing as if it were second nature. Lighting and recording the magic in such a way that their desired statement is made important. It does necessitate the knowledge of film performance and paper latitude finishes in order to enhance the end product.

Unfortunately, many 'would-be' professionals have not advanced beyond the basics of photography using their cameras simply as a mechanical paintbrush or painting by numbers. For example, they place the camera here, use such and such a focal length lens for portraits and nail the light in such a position that it is rarely moved. They perform all portraits with the same type of lighting regardless of the mood desired or age of subject. Sending out their

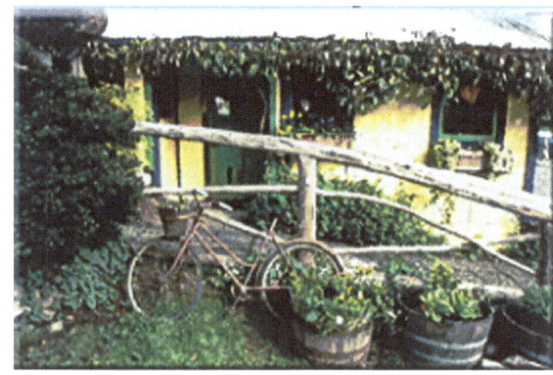

film and never giving it a second thought for the printing aspect, ie. deep or light printing, they leave it up to lab personnel who have no idea as to what mood or end result the photographer had in mind.

Talented photographers have mastered their equipment. In most cases they know exactly how they would like the subject to be presented and finished even before the button is pushed on their camera.

Like the painter, the talented photographer

has the ability to pre-visualize exactly what they want, and once the idea is born in their mind, from there on it is anti-climactic. They just need the props, to assemble their equipment accordingly, and then evoke the desired expression that they have conceptualized.

Many unimaginative photographers try to make their photographs by thinking through the camera, not giving their subject any forethought. This will only produce snapshots. The photographer performs these same pictures day after day, only changing the faces and rarely ever changes the composition. If this does occur, it is only because they are copying what they have seen produced by someone else.

Only those photographers who work by talent will perpetually compose photographs that have originality and life. Only then may they be considered a work of art. This, of course, is not inherent in everyone.

May those amongst us with a driving talent persevere their shortcomings and stand true to their calling.

Talent

It is that which cannot be taught
but yet it may be revealed

It is that which is not equal to all men
but appreciated by most

It is that which portrays beauty in its own way
but takes taste to enjoy

It is that which comes from the inner man
yet is seen in its outer parts

It is that which drives men to sacrifice
yet calls for acceptance

It is that which consumes lives
yet calls for more

It is that which is unattainable in perfection
yet it is ever striven for

- Klaus Bohn

Why Are You a Photographer?

When my three-year-old son Michael asked me the question, "Daddy, why are you a photographer and not a carpenter?" I could not answer the question fully. What are my motives? Are they pure or selfish?

Am I in it for the money which is obviously a selfish motive? Or am I in it to promote true photography for everyone? The answer did not come in a flood of inspiration. It took a great deal of soul searching, studying my motives, goals and ambitions. Perhaps this search itself is a continual evolutionary process as we grow and mature in photography.

One thing that was immediately outstanding in my mind was the privilege we have to be free. Freedom to study photography, not hemmed in to a set productivity and able to explore the facets with our individual talent, energy and goals. If we set our goals high, and a driven photographer would, perhaps never reaching maturity, we reach only our secondary objectives ripening to fruition. The discipline becomes a way of life and not merely a job to make a living.

Education

Photographic education is definitely wanting at the professional level. A person may claim to be a professional photographer without even so much as having had a correspondence course, which in itself would not produce a qualified practitioner. Some make this claim feeling justified because they own the equipment, but this is obviously unlearned thinking.

The title photographer has never been justifiably proclaimed, although more and more self-proclaimed photographers are appearing on the scene like lemmings running to self-destruction. The title 'photographer' must be earned like that of doctor, lawyer or professor. Unfortunately our social understanding of this title has lowered its worth because of the self-acclaimed photographers leaving doubt in the public mind. I might add understandably so. The salvation of this once prestigious craft or art must come first by educating the photographer, which in turn through osmosis will upgrade the value of photographers to everyone.

Objective Versus Subjective Learning

A concrete foundation or stone must be laid cementing photographers together upon a common ground. This can only come about through objective learning. In our past, we have been seduced into believing that subjective learning is the norm or only way, just because it has worked for others so it *must* work for you. At this point, I would like to clarify the meaning of objective and subjective learning.

Let's start with the latter. Subjective learning is common knowledge to most so-called photographers. Demonstrations suggest even more dramatically that it demands their expert usage of certain principles. For example, place the equipment like I do, and then you will be rewarded with this result. Another demonstration will suggest the usage of lights in another way. In this case, it may be illustrated to use only three lights like I do, use only one and reflect it in the same way as I do, or use eight lights and place them exactly this way.

Never enlightening the photographer with what the light is or does because of the way the light is used, the individual is not much the wiser. I am not degrading the value of learning via subjective teaching, but rather its premature usage. A child cannot learn to run before they have learned to walk. Before the beginner can comprehend what the demonstrator is teaching, they must first have a common ground of understanding.

Objective learning lays the foundation. The instructor that has the capability to teach what light does, for example, can then advance to multiple lights and what they accomplish. Additionally, they may then advise about the different types of lights used such as parabolic, umbrella, natural, etc., and their end results. Similarly, various lenses may be shown and guidance provided as to their end results, as well as their effect upon a scene may be discussed. Learning the effect of certain materials or equipment and their respective usage leaves the photographer better informed and educated. Then they are able to put together what they envision the end result should be from understanding the effect of the material and equipment used.

In objective learning processes, the photographer is allowed to use their own imagination through an understandable usage of materials. Consequently, each photographer may use different equipment and light that they have envisioned, producing an end result in a unique and individualized manner rather than copying a demonstrator.

Learning the various effects of light will not restrict us in its usage. Whereas copying a demonstrator restricts us in using the light exactly the same way as we were taught, thus limiting our imagination. The various possibilities that we might have been able to use to portray our subject were restricted.

I would like to interject at this point and mention why I feel we have been bombarded with only subjective learning. Firstly, our instructors are definitely unqualified to teach objectively. Secondly, the labs tend to dictate to most photographers that their job would be easier if we all expose our negatives the same way. To play the game then, we must follow the rules that appear to be in authority. Relinquishing our freedom to understand photography and its materials, we are then enslaved to the standards imposed by a lab.

It Is Not About the Camera

It always amuses me when I see someone carrying a camera with a long lens around their neck walk into my studio browsing. They look at my images as if they can appreciate what I have done in just a glance or a few seconds at best. I always wonder what is going through their mind. Is it all about the equipment they are carrying?

Just the other day I had a video director come in due to an image I had in the window. He said that it arrested his attention. He came back and looked at the photo again then came in and wants to use it for the cover of his video cassette. When he had a few minutes I observed *how* he looked at the portraits I had in my gallery. He really looked, took time and then expressed his observation and feelings. To my amazement he said that he had studied photography for a couple of years and had looked at many images, but had not seen many with the attention that these photographs brought to him.

A number of years ago when I first wanted to teach I was told that my class should have a name. I did not mull over this request light heartedly, but with great focus if you will pardon the pun. I needed something that could stand the test of time so a slogan was born, **"Feeling more deeply about photography"** not realizing that down the road it would be known as a "brand." A brand is not what one does necessarily, but rather what we are all about. For me, it is to pass on this involvement in the art of photography. Hence the name of my studio, **Photographic Art**. The impressions that we make and leave behind for others to view and study not just once, but hopefully often and forever.

What is photography? An expression of one's view perhaps, but much more than that embodying statement. Is it a lifetime of studying, looking and observing with our heart where talent lives? Is it about the person, the so-called artist? Their whole life is represented in their work. We can't separate who we are from what we do if we are truly an artist! Even when my words fail me and my image fails me, my heart is always true. The longer I look at my work the more of myself I can recognize. It has nothing to do with like or dislike, but rather it is what the true image is, the reflection or mirror image which is opposite to my view of reality.

The more I mature the more truth lies within one's life and work. It cannot be counterfeited or copied because when it is copied the feeling of reality is not there. We need to be true to ourselves in this struggle of a lifetime. When all is said and done, what is left behind is the memory, our work and who we were. These may be embellished over and over again and that is the true test of time, in the imagination of others. May we not roll over in our graves.

Can You be a Photographer?

A myriad of sources would make this suggestion most vehemently. Everyone is bombarded day after day with pictures from every direction. We live in a picture world, conditioning everyone with images that in themselves are at best mediocre.

Equipment manufacturers are geared for the amateur market. Automated cameras that you aim and fire lull everyone into the dream world of being a photographer. Camera and film manufacturers have made preposterous acclaim or blame regarding equipment and materials. One such advertisement was showing a monkey taking pictures. This is an insult to every camera buff, let alone the professional. Think about it.

The crime of cheating on what is true photography, while not punishable, has been all but buried beneath sophomoric logic that everyone has the potential to be a photographer. What may we then consider the make-up of a true photographer?

Knowing one's equipment as if it were an extension of ourselves is no more than to be expected. Understanding light and the effect of it is a definite prerequisite in becoming a photographer in order to reveal mood, feeling and a message to the viewer. Understanding the history of photography and where it has been, is a necessity in order that we can have direction in our work with significant historical continuance and dedication. To have that all consuming drive, to make photography of consequence for all time and understandable to everyone, this is important!

If we stop here, we still have not reached the nub of truth in photography. That something inside us, which we refer to as "talent" and not mere intellect which goes beyond this and that, is not inherent to everyone. That special something that has always separated the true artistic person from the counterfeit is needed in order to be classified as a "Photographer."

The Importance of Composition

Our eyes like to follow eye lines. For example, if I look up long enough other people walking by will also look up. We prefer to follow leading lines like finger pointing or eye lines i.e. where the eye is looking.

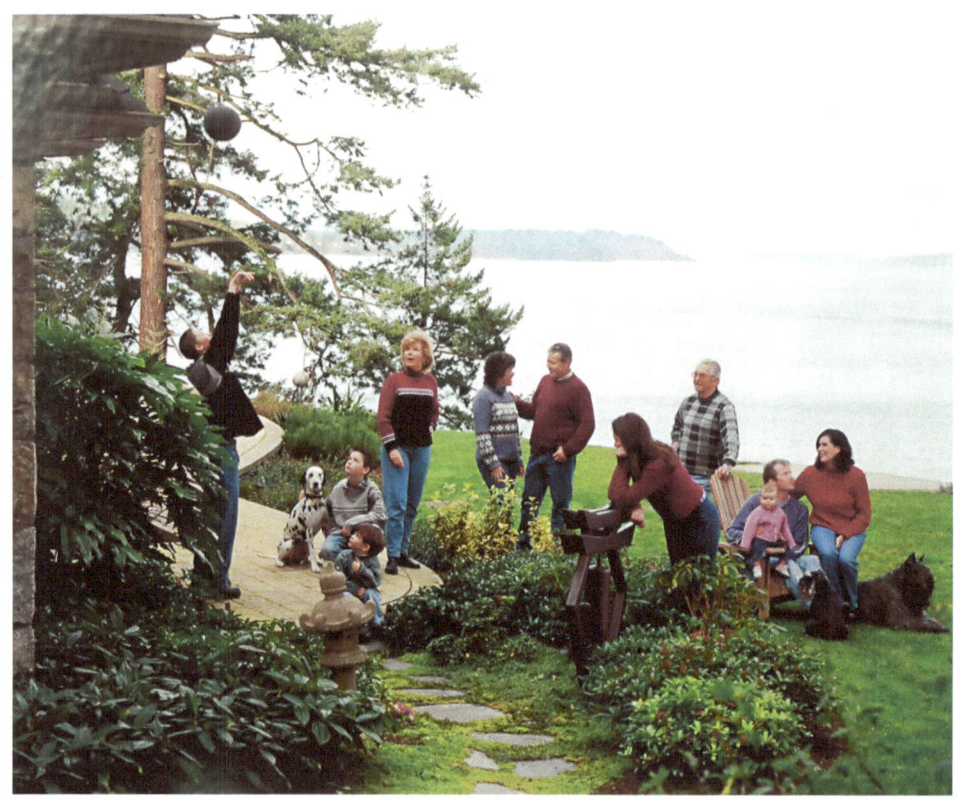

The image above illustrates the movement of where each person is looking. We can then get involved with the inner action of the image and see pictures within the overall image. This enables the viewer to study the storytelling event before leaving the photograph.

The dog on the left with the path in front brings the viewer's eye into the image quickly and easily. Also, the little girl on the right will bring us back again because she is looking at us.

Like music, the rhythm and movement of the composition adds tempo and interest so that we not only look, but also study what is happening in this family group. When we chunk each element down to just a fragment of the whole, we can see many images in one. Storytelling visually can be very simple or complex depending on the artist's vision and talent.

50 Principles of Composition

1. Moving in Close

Amateur photographers often include unnecessary elements that do not add to the statement or meaning of the photograph. By **_moving in close_**, we can eliminate at least most of that which has no relevance to the storytelling feature. In most cases, this eliminates at least 85% of the photographic area in most amateurs' pictures. Their snapshots will then improve immensely.

Learn to use "L's" when reviewing each photograph as in the small picture below. Learning to do this will help you see more photographically. The acronym KISS should be applied here: "Keep It Simple Stupid." This is sound advice, worthwhile adhering to.

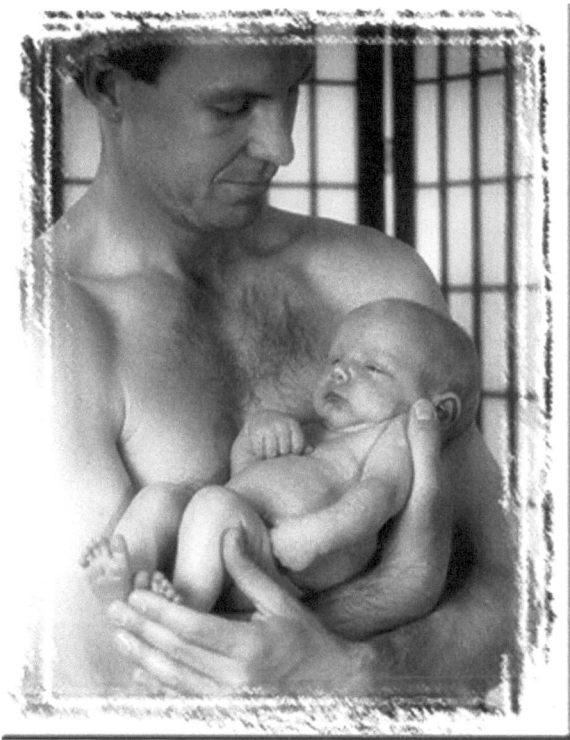

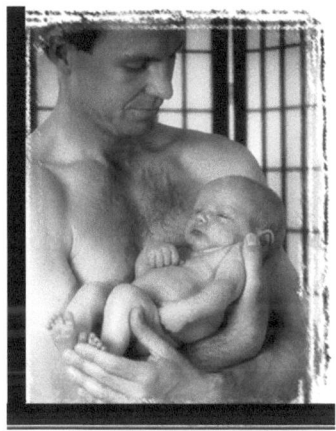

2. Placing Center of Interest

The "dead center syndrome" of placing everything of importance in the immediate center should be avoided. This is the most static and boring placement in the entire format. Unless we are trying to communicate boredom, it is better to place the center of interest in a stronger location. By dividing your format into thirds you can alleviate the tendency to put the subject in the middle of the frame. The diagram below indicates the four alternative focal points to use as guides.

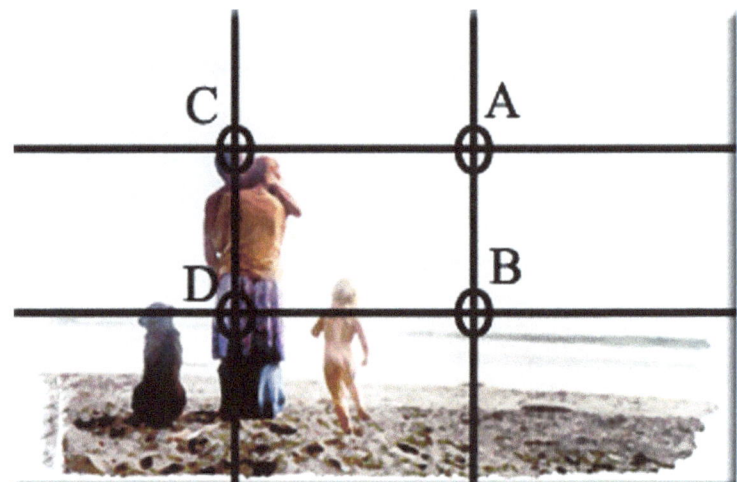

In the Western World, people have been conditioned to read from left to right. Consequently, "A" is perhaps the strongest focal point, followed in order by "B", then "C" and the weakest "D".

This principle involving thirds has evolved from one used in painting for centuries known as "The Golden Mean." Painters, however, use the ratio of 5:8 instead of thirds.

3. Placing Secondary Objects

Place recording objects in proper relation to the main one(s). The format may now be divided into sixths, sometimes referred to as fifths, and these intersections, illustrated below as pink lines, then become a secondary interest.

For example, a car that is movable in relationship to a house should be placed at a camera angle in the 1/6 vicinity. Careful consideration must be given to proper placement at the secondary intersections while keeping in mind that the result can give one a feeling of motion, tension, excitement, etc., that is not inherent in all photographs.

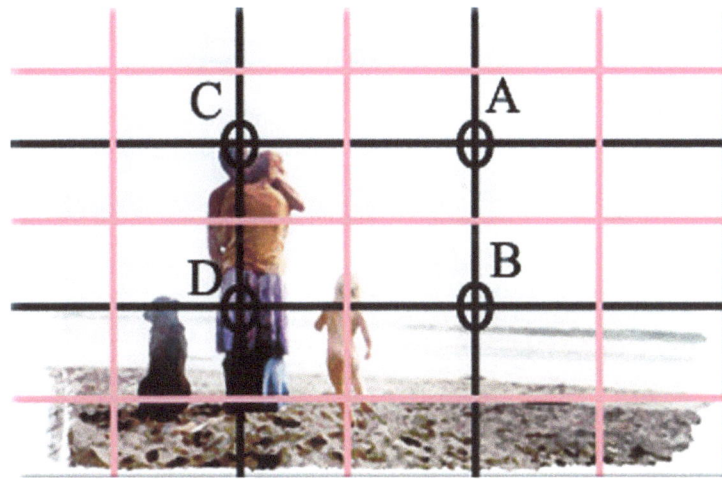

4. "Framing" the Photograph

"Frame" the picture with trees, rocks, hills, and so on. That will act as a bumper or stopper, forcing the eye back onto the main subject. When viewing a photograph "framed" by a tree on either side, our eyes find it psychologically hard to "go through" the tree and run out of the photo. In reality, this is of course an impossibility.

Psychological *tricks* such as the one mentioned can be an aid when trying to keep the eye in the photo. Remember that what we have experienced in the past will have a lasting and ingrained influence on our psychological encounters.

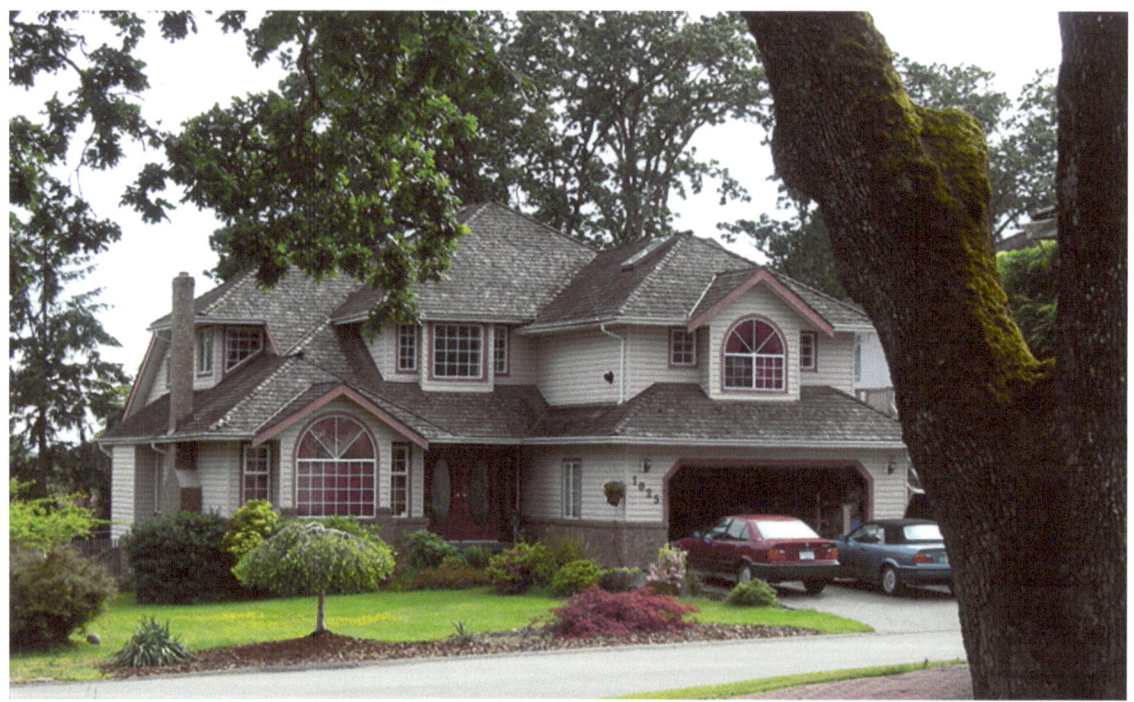

5. Dividing the Photograph

When "dividing the photograph," the most static division as mentioned would be the center. The object would be divided into two equal parts. However, if one is saying that the scene is to be static and boring, by all means divide your photograph in the middle. A desert scene and grey sky with nothing but the same for miles on end could be photographed like this.

When looking down on something, usually the object should occupy the bottom of the photo. Likewise, if we are looking up at something, it should usually occupy the top portion of the photo. Our eyes demand continuity.

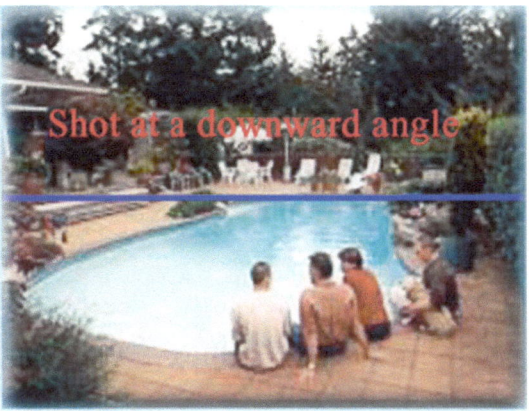

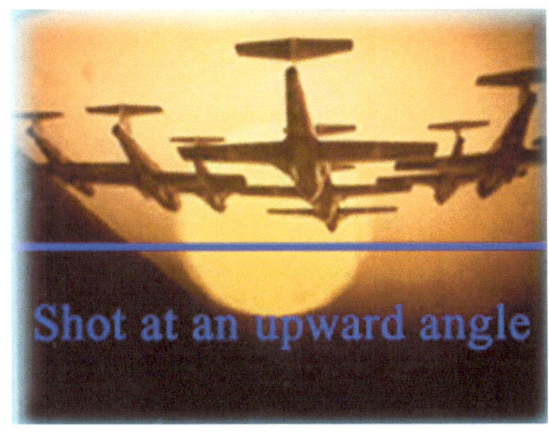

6. Separating the Subject and Background

Overlapping objects should be avoided, such as trees growing out of people's heads. This is unnatural and undesirable. The photographer should provide a separation through placement or lighting between the subject and its background. By removing the object behind the subject, by removing the subject from the location, or by using a higher or lower camera angle, the photograph can usually be improved upon.

Viewing from unique angles most often gives the viewer greater impact as they have not experienced that before, not consciously at least to this point. Once we are aware of these possibilities we begin to explore, and that is part of photography. Enjoy the exploration of this great discipline of image making.

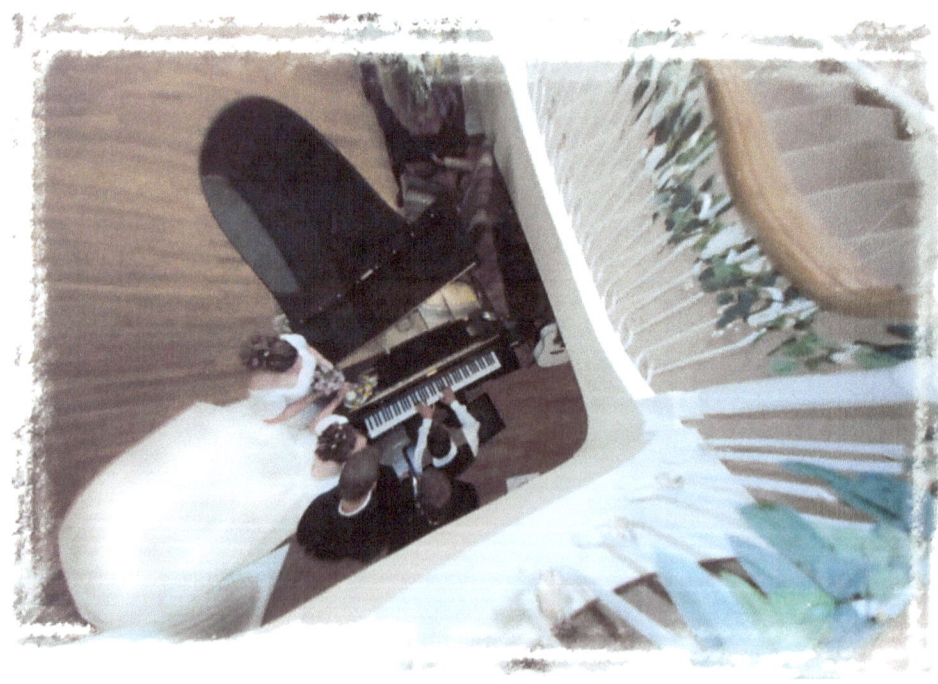

7. Avoiding Mental Hazards

Avoid mental hazards or "road blocks." These are obstructions to the center of interest and may be a deterrent, keeping the eye from staying in the photograph. An example might be a fence running across the photo preventing the eye from entering into the same scene and lingering long enough to enjoy the effect. We should try to make it as easy as possible to allow the eye to enter into and remain in the photograph as long as possible.

Capturing the eye, so to speak, for a few seconds longer can enhance the beauty of the image to the viewer psychologically. This can remain with us longer because of our emotional feelings, what is in the heart, the heart of the mind! And yet there are exceptions to every rule.

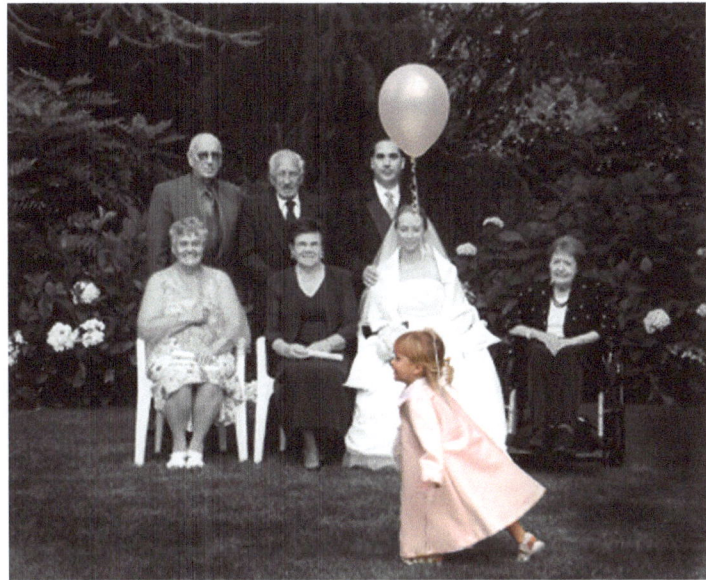

In this image the family was posed and just as I was taking the picture this little girl who was full of life ran across the scene. To most, the balloon and string results in an awkward image that detracts from the bride and groom. However, in this instance the family did not see the balloon and string as a visual distraction, but rather an enhancement of the little girl's innocence and a moment frozen in time. In fact, the family ordered this image in a large 20 by 24 inch print for their wall.

8. Balancing for Harmony

The simplest form of balance is with both halves of a photograph possessing the same object mass and being symmetrically located.

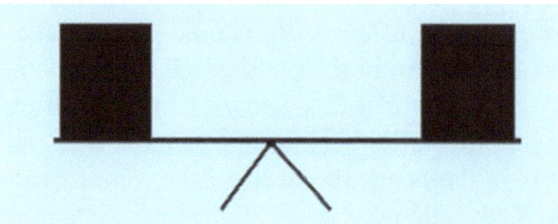

The two objects above appear to be the same size and weight, being placed at either end of the table. They would of course have balance. They also have a boring and static look. By adding what would appear to be imbalance to the objects, a new feeling is created. For instance, dark colours have more weight psychologically than lighter coloured objects.

Also, from our experiences, in a psychological sense, what seems to be light in weight when compared to another object that is heavier in weight can create an imbalance.

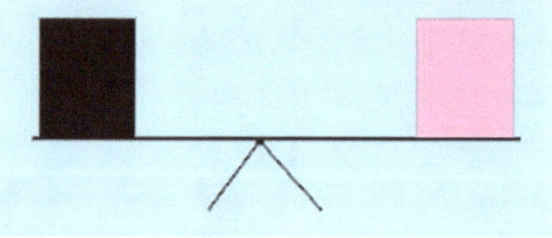

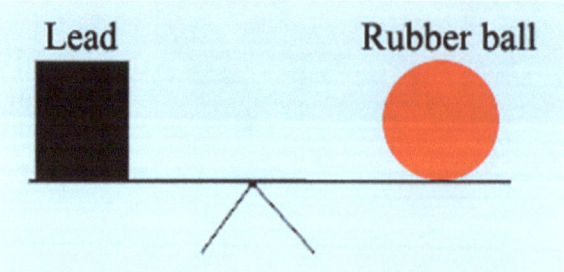

These imbalances add tension and a feeling of motion in our minds. By moving the fulcrum, illustrated by the person depicted below, closer to the heavier looking object, the house, a feeling of harmony and better balance can be created.

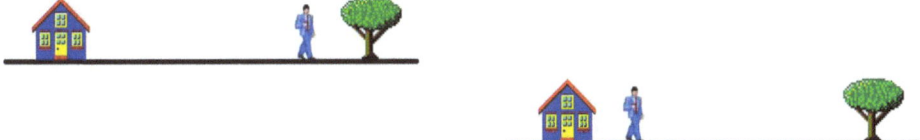

By composing imbalance psychologically, or balance physically, harmony and excitement can be established in your photographs.

9. Choosing Vertical or Horizontal Formats

Choosing vertical or horizontal formats can be difficult for the novice photographer to appreciate. A simple suggestion is that vertical formats seem to express dignity, and give proud upright expressions. Strength and grandeur are noted in choices such as trees, towers and executive-type portraits. Keep in mind that the vertical format can also give a static, formal effect.

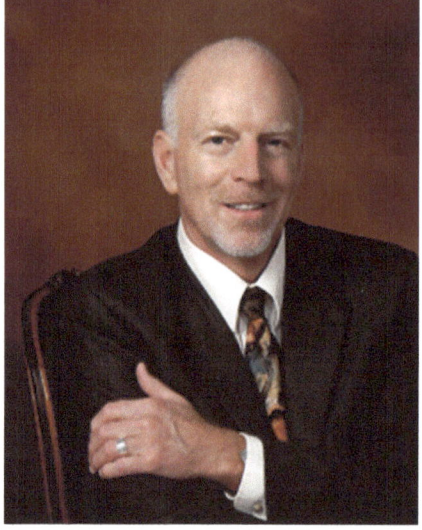

Horizontal framing helps to suggest peace, quiet and restfulness, as well as an overall

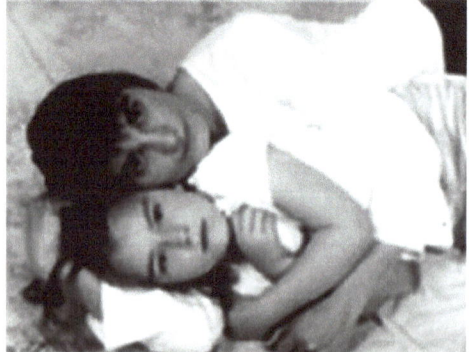

balance. A couple examples are a quiet lake scene or a stretched out body sleeping peacefully. This format has a feminine quality of beauty to it.

10. Leading Lines

Lines, like roads, rivers and branches of trees suggest different feelings such as grandeur, repose, action and beauty. Lines can possess emotional qualities. Curved lines are soothing and pleasing, jagged lines are explosive in quality, vertical lines are dignifying, horizontal lines are restful and serene, and diagonal lines are lively and active. For example, consider a lower horizontal line for spaciousness in your photographs, and higher ones to suggest closeness.

The lines can be leading lines to the main object for the eye to follow. A continuous line like a circle may keep the eye in a revolving movement and consequently, keep the eye in the scene longer.

Not all lines necessarily have to be actual lines, they may be suggested. An eye line when someone is looking at something is one example. Their eye is a suggestive body line causing your own eye to follow theirs to the main object in the photograph. This photo, as mentioned before, is an ideal illustration because it has examples of various actual lines as well as a few suggested lines.

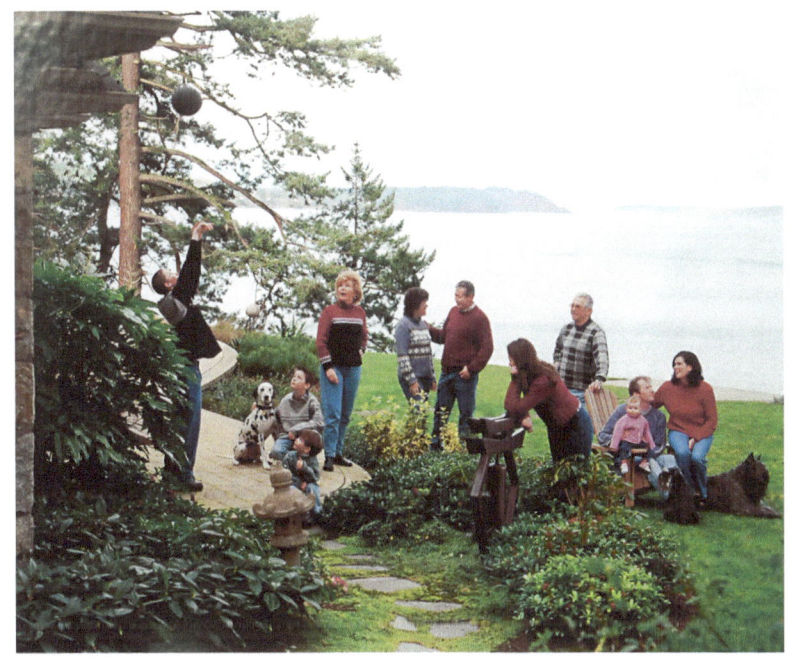

11. Moving Objects

The treatment of moving objects is important. Give space for the object to move into. It is far better to leave enough space in front of a moving object. That way the object doesn't appear as though it will bump into the outer edge of the photograph. If a person is running and they are at the outer edge turning their head back, then their eye line can bring us back into the photograph.

It is even more acceptable to have the subject run or jump into a photograph than to run out of it. If a horse is jumping into the photo over a hurdle, cut off his tail or a back foot to suggest movement.

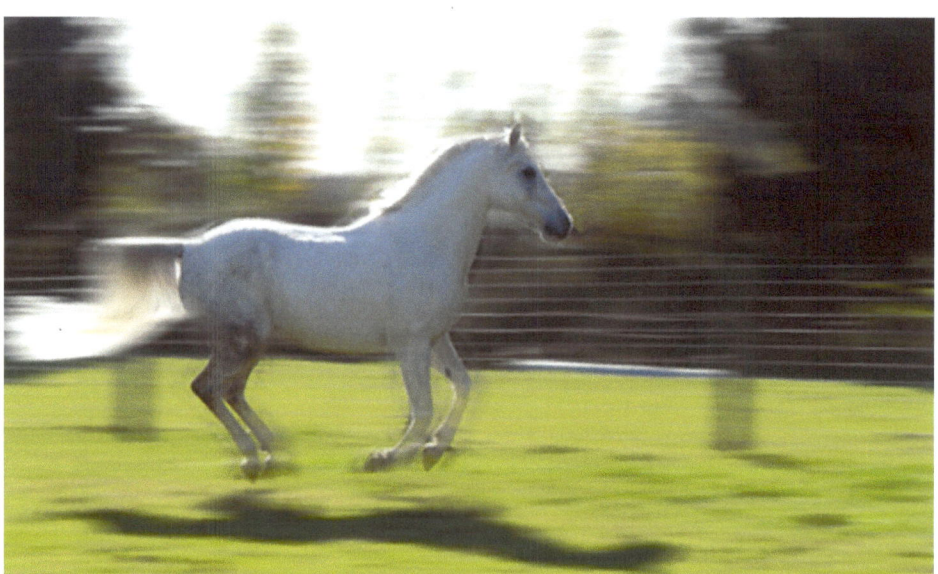

12. Placing People

Consider the placement of a person in a scenic photograph in such a way that a semi-portait within a scene is not created. Your eyes are torn between looking at the person and looking at the scene.

A suggestion is to size the person in a scene no larger than 1/4 the total size of the photo. This can envelope a person into a scene rather than creating two focal points competing for the main point of interest. Perhaps the person could even be looking into the scene rather than at the camera, which has a tendency to make it more of a pictorial study.

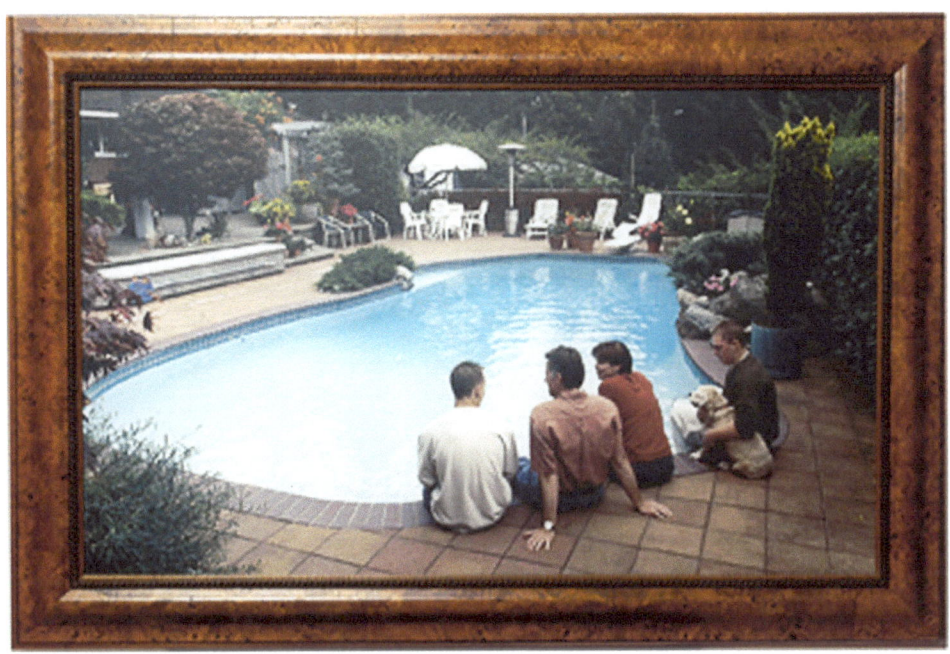

13. Centralization of Religious Symbols

  Religious symbols may demand more centralization because of the spiritual qualities. A cross or church in dead center of the photo is an example. The cross gives the feeling of force, unity and harmony.

  Lines in one direction are monotonous. They need a transitional or additional line to give relationship to the whole composition. Attention will be attracted to the place where the two lines cross. The intersections or crossing lines should not occur too near the frame.

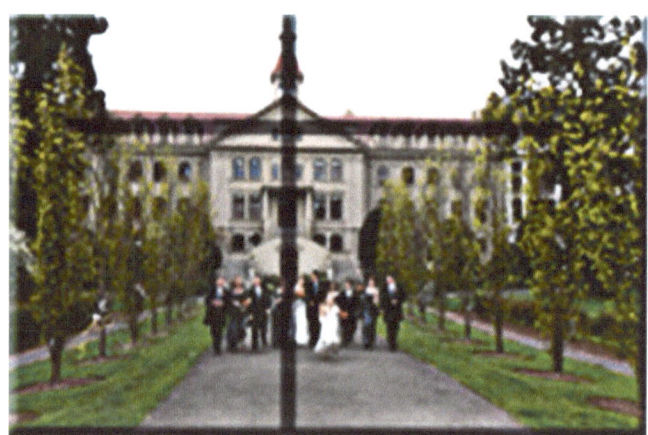

14. Colour Composition

Colour composition on its own could fill several books. Basically cold colours such as blue and green recede, while warm colours such as red and yellow advance. Therefore, by manipulating our colour with this in mind, we can add the illusion of depth. Once again it is advisable under most circumstances to not divide a photograph into equal parts and the same applies to colour.

With a red barn and green grass, the most pleasing ratio would be 80:20 or 90:10 and not 50:50. The eye psychologically accommodates itself to the scene, and in so doing reduces our ability to see exactly what is in front of us. Film reproduces what it 'sees', while its rendition of a particular colour may differ considerably from our mental comprehension of it.

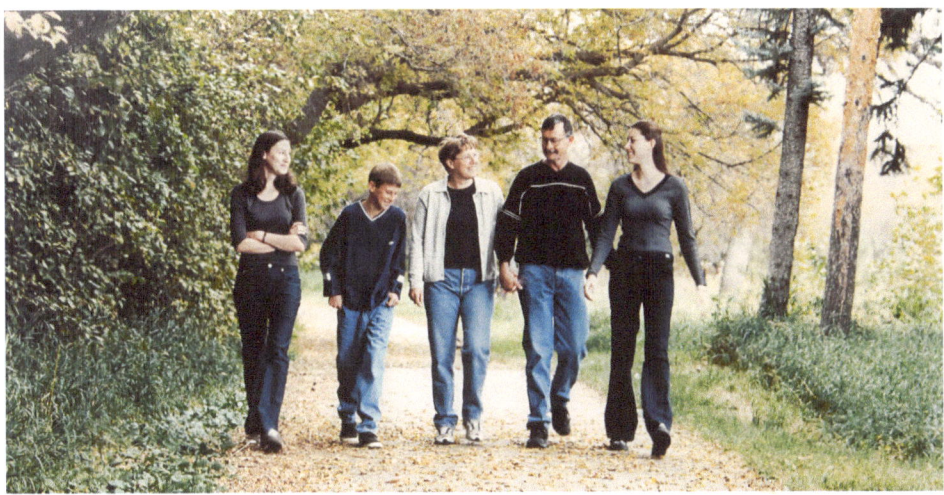

In the above image the green foliage gives the impression of receding or being in the background, thereby adding extra emphasis and impact to the subjects.

15. Filters

Filters on the camera can add reality and depth. Natural fog adds distance to the photograph, and by adding a fog filter, we may change the illusion of depth. Other filters can change the appearance of reality into being either more or less real.

There is a myriad of filters with each having its own effect on the photograph i.e. cross stars, repeaters, colour filters, etc. When one views the Rocky Mountains from Calgary in the fog, they look farther away than they do on a clear day. By adding the fog filter, this illusion of depth may be created at will.

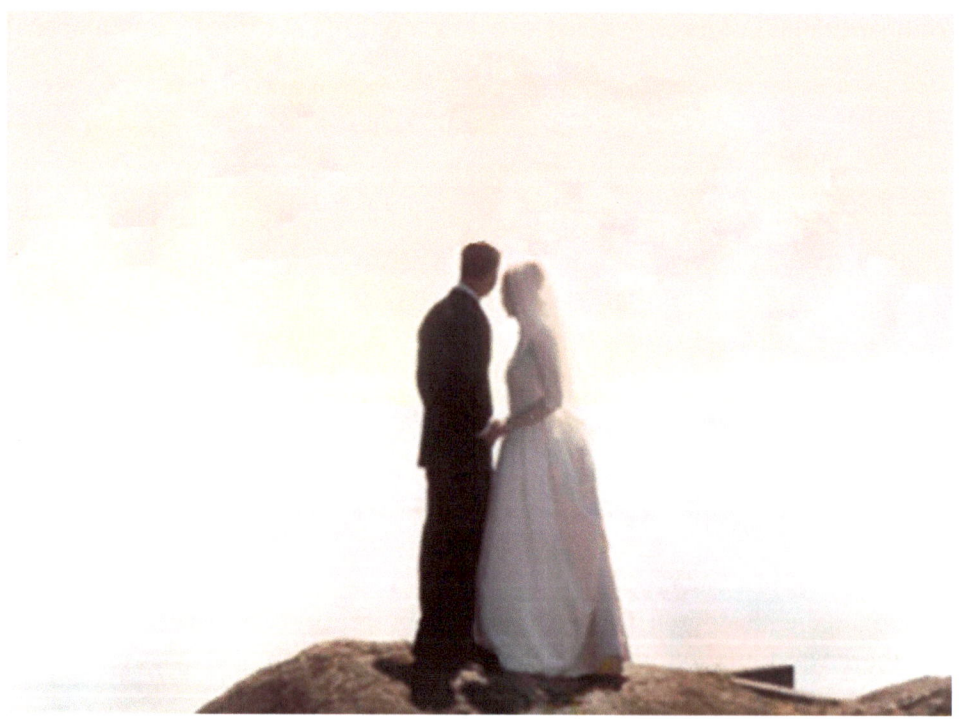

16. Avoiding Center of Interest

We do not always need a center of interest. There are times when the whole photograph has no one particular focal point. One example could be coloured leaves in a heap. To many, they look like a tapestry of colour and as such no focal point is needed. Another example would be cracked, parched earth during a dry spell or drought, or crashing waves along a shore line as illustrated below.

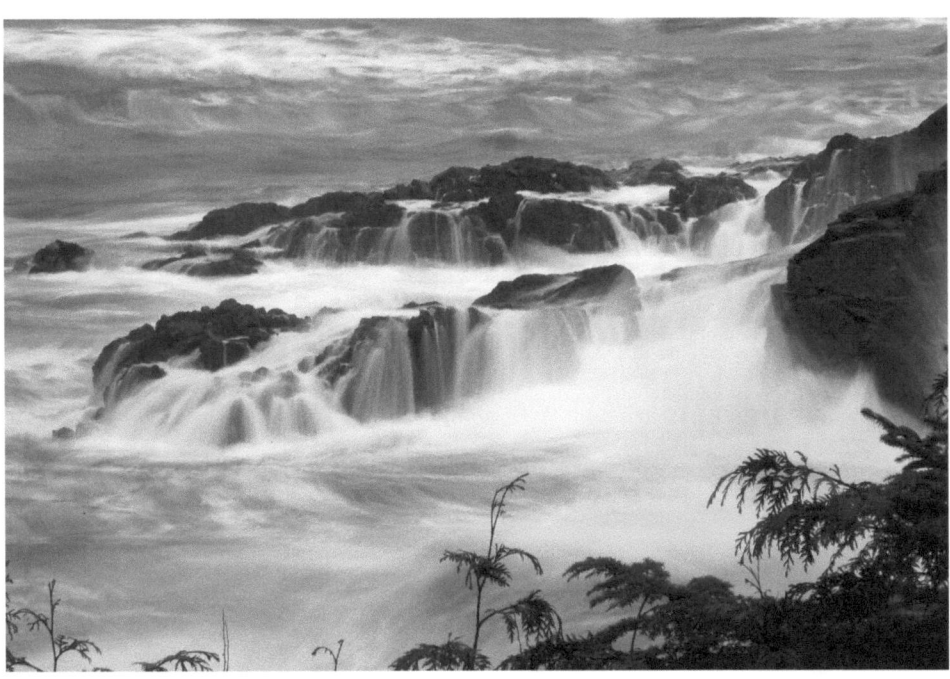

17. Suggesting What is Not Apparent

Using tricks of imagination adds to a photograph in suggesting what apparently may be there. You may be trying to suggest a group of factory workers going to work in a factory that is in the distance even though there are only three people walking to work. By cutting off the last person's hand or back, one could suggest that there are others behind him also going to work.

Like the horse photo presented in Principle 11, Moving Objects, we are suggesting, or not, that there are other horses trying to catch up. Look at other photos throughout this book to try and find other examples. Even the principles that have no image directly associated with them can be found illustrated in other photos. Keep this in mind as you read these pages and use your eyes to see what is not apparent on first glance. This is an exercise on its own!

18. Fore-, Middle and Background

   To add reality through the illusion of depth, we need to keep in mind the three grounds that we are given to use: foreground, middle ground and background. Omitting one or any combination of these grounds takes away from seeing reality in a photograph, unless it is made up in some other way through light or some other principle of composition.

   The **foreground** is the part of the scene that is in front of you and closest to the camera. The **background** includes the more distant part of the scene, such as sky, a wall or foliage. The **middle ground** is the part of the picture that lies between the two extremes. An effective way to achieve a strong feeling of depth in a photograph is to include all three: fore-, middle and background.

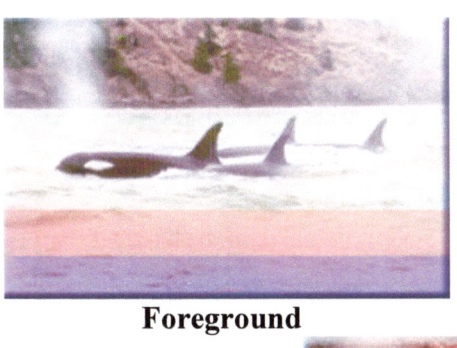
Foreground

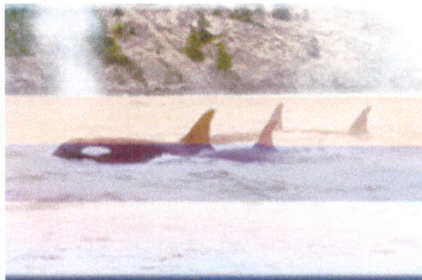
Middle Ground

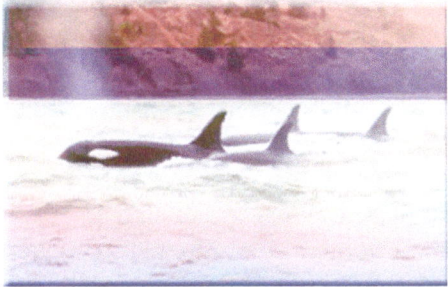
Background

19. Rhythm

Repetition of objects or lines gives rhythm or swing to a picture. It helps to establish a definite pattern or quality which aids in expressing moods or feelings. Too much repetition evenly spread out can be rhythmic.

In most photographs the spacing is accentuated freely. Free rhythm is a pleasing uneven spacing. Repetition of angles is especially good. Variations of size, spacing and contrast could be used, but not to the point of being too varied. Try to keep a beat with variety in order to make the repetition interesting. When shapes are rhythmically repeated to form an overall design, you finish with a pattern.

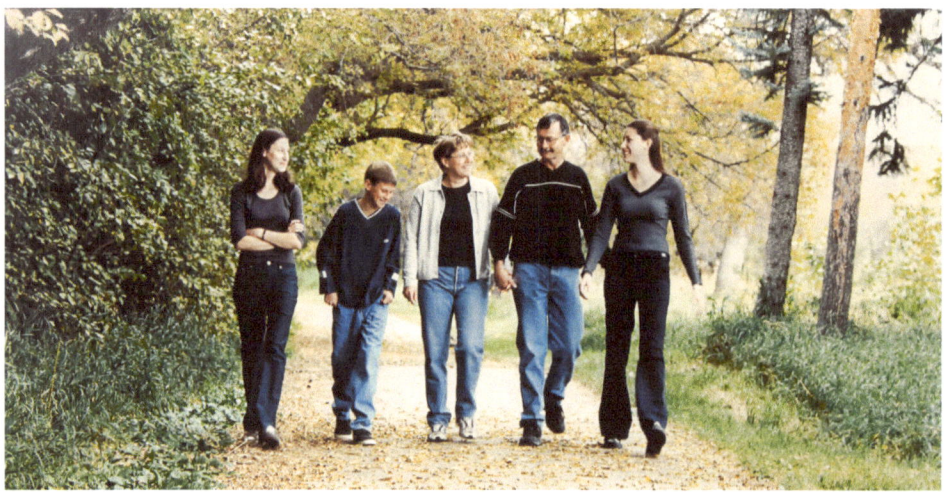

The family pictured above represents a rhythm or swing in their movements as they are walking along the trail. This image has been repeated to illustrate that many photos have multiple compositional elements interacting simultaneously. A photographer who carefully plans or pre-visualizes their photos can harmoniously balance the subjects in the photo within the space around them.

20. Texture

Texture is related to rhythm and patterns as an element of composition. Photographers should be very much aware of textures and how to handle them photographically.

Texture is actually a small scale pattern that reveals the surface qualities of an object. Photography is unsurpassed in its ability to render texture in detail. The roughness of tree bark or roads, the softness of silk, the sheen of metal or the smoothness of flesh, all can be shown in your pictures. Emphasize the unique quality of different textures for the powerful effects they can make.

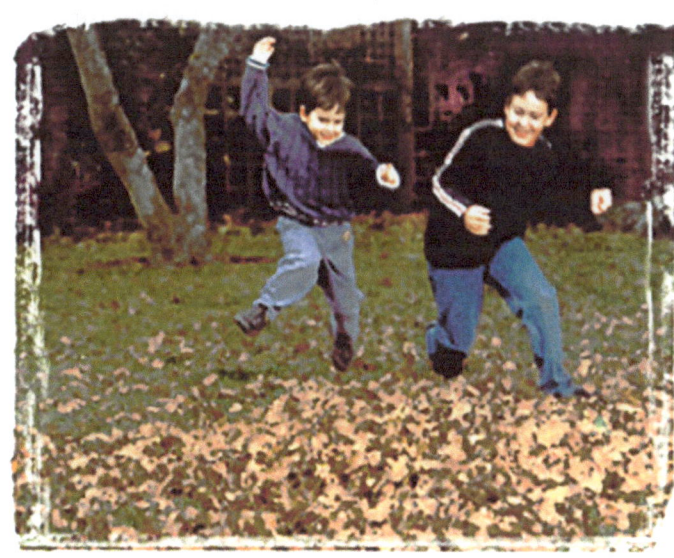

The roughness of the fallen leaves against the seemingly smoother green grass are just two of the many different textures being shown in the image with the two boys at play.

21. Omitted Items

What we leave out may be the most important item or message in the photograph. The empty square in the following diagram draws more attention than all the other filled squares.

Consider this technique for a dramatic photo!

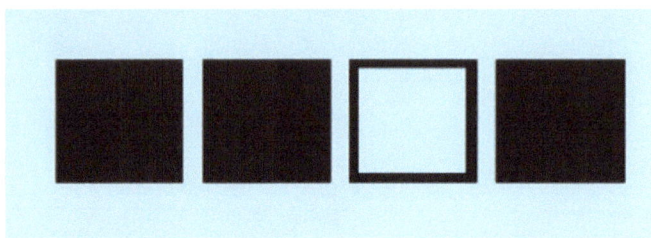

22. Space

Concepts about space should be considered. A photograph can give the illusion of flattened art, picture space or the illusion of depth. Although the scene of three-dimensional space that we sense in a photograph is an illusion, nevertheless photographic space affects us emotionally and we respond to it.

By considering the positive space occupied by our subjects in the photo and the negative space occupied by empty space, even the negative space has mass weight. Limited space gives the feeling of intimacy or confinement, or sometimes a mixture of both. It can suggest closeness, comfort, intimacy, tightness, imprisonment or a feeling of claustrophobia.

When we speak about planes in a photo, it is important to remember that planes are not always solid. Planes can be perforated as in the case with screen doors, fences and windows. Some planes are implied as with a row of objects going over a hill. A plane can be nothing more than a thin row of trees on the edge of a pond.

There are occasions when the monocular vision of the camera affects the rendering of depth. Space can be collapsed or telescoped. When it is telescoped the subject may appear to shift in space from near to far. Parts pop in and out, or they fluctuate in space. Fluctuating space lacks both the intimate feeling of limited space and the nostalgia of deep space. It produces a kind of strange, shifting and insecure feeling in the view.

23. Value Contrast

Value contrast in black and white or colour can emphasize the values you choose them to be ie. solid, exciting, dramatic, gentle, soothing, peaceful, sad or happy. Look for the positive versus negative responses in your total range, as referred to in Principle 22, Space. Dark, light and mid-tonal values are extremely important in photographic composition.

Dark values such as shadows and blackness can be associated with night, death or the unknown. They can also seem mournful, mysterious, dignified, peaceful or masculine. Light values such as white and light greys tend to be used to signify sunlight, gaiety, youth, frivolity, delicateness and femininity.

Emphasis on clarity and definition can be based on a simple principle. The greater the value contrast the more distinct the definition, and the greater the emphasis, especially when dealing in black and white. In colour, you need to allow for the progressive and regressive response of additive and subtractive.

Strive for contrast in shape and size, contrasts in colour or light and dark. Shadows, especially long deep ones give a feeling of mystery. This feeling can be intensified with a low horizon. The circle and a pyramid or triangle are the forms over which an amateur has most control. Other forms are the radii, cross, rectangles and the 'L' shape. An example of a cross formation was illustrated in the image accompanying Principle 13, Centralization of Religious Symbols.

24. Circles

A circle gives the sensation of continued movement and is used a great deal in 'framing'. The imaginative circular frame formed by darker areas near the edges help to keep the eye in the picture as it revolves around the center of interest. Avoid light areas at the edge of the picture except where the eyes enter the frame. The circle can also be used in the grouping of objects or points of interest within the frame.

Many objects, of course, are round, and leading lines in a picture may be circular as the shore line of a small lake within a scene.

As can be seen in this photograph, the tree and foliage 'frame' the center of interest. The frame is circular and thus draws your eyes into the picture.

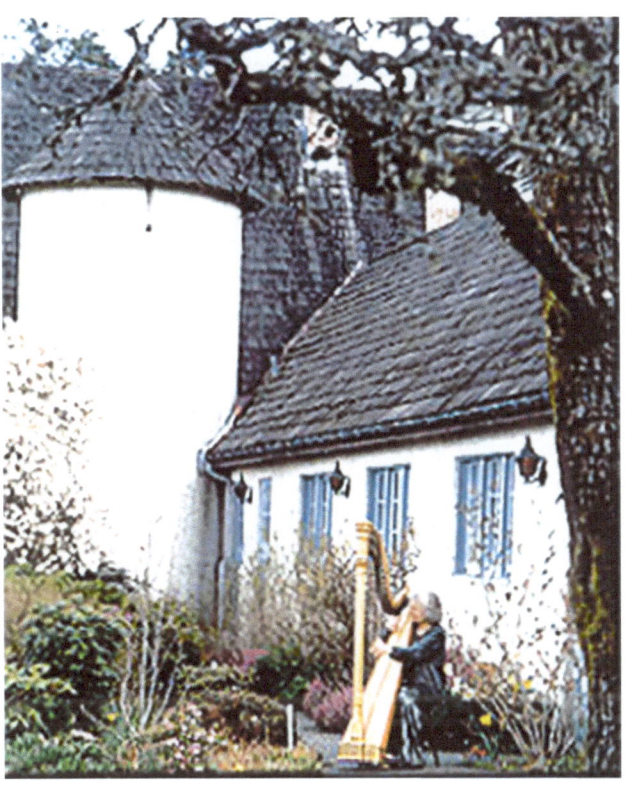

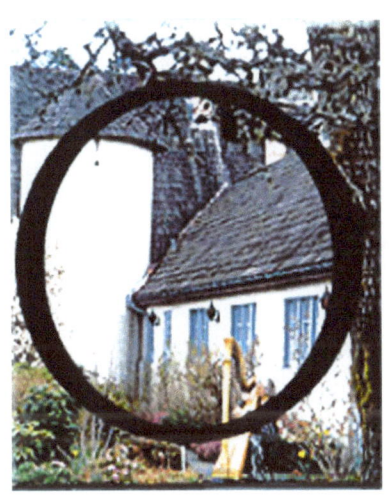

25. Pyramids

The pyramid or triangle is the most important of the fundamental forms and is the most widely used. It is found in almost all compacted designs. The pyramid gives strength, design and stability to a composition and leads to a climax. Like a circle, it is easy for the eye to follow. Large trees, mountain peaks and most tall buildings arranged in groups are ready-made examples.

The pyramid can be used to great advantage in portraits and in the grouping of objects or figures. In portraits, the elbows may be extended from the body as the subject rests them on a table or other object. A girl can sit on a log and lean on her outstretched arm. A child sitting on the floor usually assumes a carefree pyramidal pose.

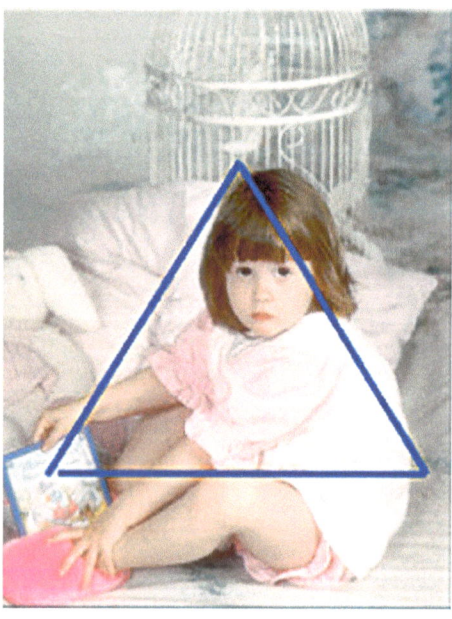 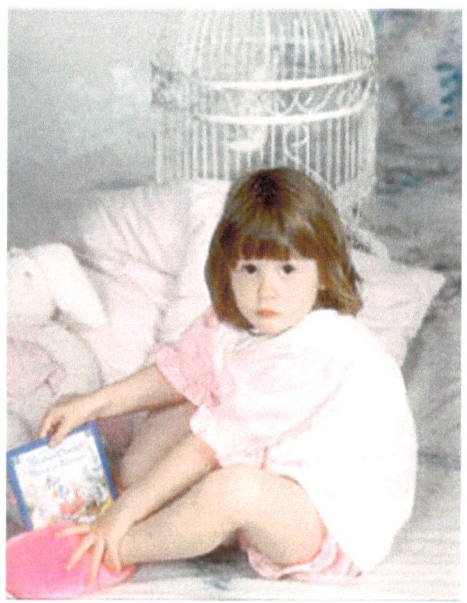

When you group objects or figures, the tallest and most important is usually placed near the center. Keep the pyramid in mind when you make such arrangements. The great masters used the triangle composition in most of their great religious paintings. These paintings make a very interesting study.

Composition in Hindsight

At this halfway point in the 50 principles of composition, let's stop to reflect on the origins of composition in art. It is important to learn from the great artists of the past and to discover how they used their vision to see and represent objects on canvas using paints. My favourite painter is Thomas Gainsborough (1727-1788), an English painter of portraits, landscapes, and elegant pictures. He is considered one of the most individual geniuses in British art.

I fell in love with his use of space when I visited one of Europe's finest galleries in Berlin. I stood for a very long time and viewed a large painting of Gainsborough's entitled, "Mr. and Mrs. Andrews" (1750), which had a very unique way of using space. The curator walked over to me and asked, "Would you like me to tell you about the artist and why he painted the way he did?" He had my full attention, of course, and he proceeded to tell me that Gainsborough liked to paint scenery. In order to sell his paintings to the rich, it was necessary to include people. The wealthy merchants and famous people of the day could afford to pay him what he needed to live.

The painting took on a special dimension that enthralled me to use this concept in my own work. To show space and keeping in mind that people needed to be an appropriate size, the image needed to be an appropriate size as well. Some of the images I have done have been commissions up to 40 by 70 inches, which is very large in portrait photography. The best selling sizes have been 30 by 40 inches and 24 by 36 inches. All this resulted because I had the opportunity to not only see the Gainsborough collection but to also learn from what the curator told me about his use of space.

Gainsborough's 1748 painting entitled, "The Charterhouse," as well as the teachings of the late Rocky Gunn assisted in my understanding and use of circles in the composition of my photographs. Rocky once said, "Klaus, don't just use pyramids, also use circles within the image." The beauty about using circles within an image, even the outer dimensions of the image having a circular frame, is that it can provide a fresh impact to the viewer.

Additionally, Gainsborough's 1770 painting entitled "The Blue Boy," has a warm muted background which is contrasted by the blue outfit worn by the young boy. It helped in my understanding and use of warm backgrounds more readily than before, and that the subject's clothing need not be indicative of the background colour. Finally, I also appreciated Gainsborough's 1751-2 oil on canvas entitled "Thomas Gainsborough, with His Wife and

Elder Daughter Mary," as it shows a need to photograph our families in the way we envision our relationship with them.

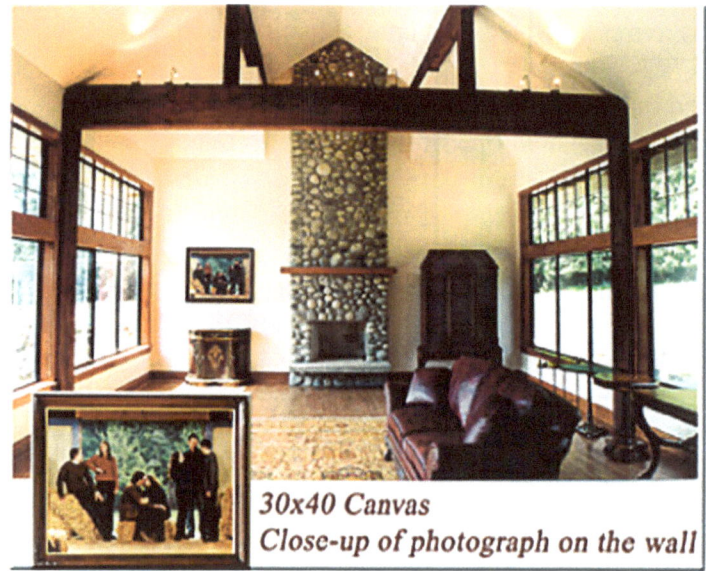

30x40 Canvas
Close-up of photograph on the wall

Pictured at left is a clipping of a brochure we made that had a tremendous response from potential clients.

Another favourite artist of mine is Rembrandt (1606-1669), generally considered one of the greatest painters in European art history and the most important in Dutch history. In his oil on canvas from 1642 entitled "The Night Watch" (The Militia Company of Captain Frans Banning Cocq and of Lieutenant Willem van Ruytenburgh), he uses light and shadows, people looking in different directions with some faces not even seen, and emotions varying from person to person. I like the concept of everyone looking naturally unposed. Rembrandt departed from the traditional formal portrait genre and instead used his imagination and creativity in composing this image. Not everyone is looking at the paintbrush, so to speak.

Rembrandt's self portraits illustrate an exercise that a lot of artists have pursued. I have been encouraged to do the same and have always highly recommended this study of self to be an ongoing lifelong pursuit for all photographers. Pictured here is a self portrait I did several years ago. My son David has been faithful in this endeavour as well.

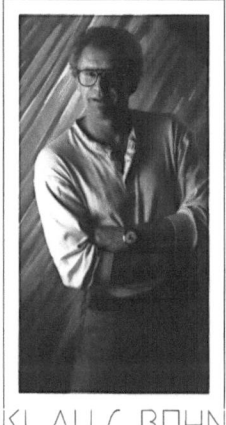

KLAUS BOHN

In photography we are conditioned to always look at the camera when we are having our picture taken. However, very seldom do you see portraits composed by exploring new avenues by having the subject look away from the lens of a camera. Additionally, in searching out the individuality and seeing how impressions change, we do not need to light everyone the same way. It is important to learn from the past, from the great ones, and understand how liberated they seemed to be. My personal ambition is not to be afraid.

Mona Lisa is a 16th century oil painting on poplar wood by Leonardo da Vinci, and is one of the most famous paintings in Western art history. When viewing this painting in person, I stood and stared for a very long time. I was truly in awe, spellbound and transfixed as if I was immovable. To stand in the presence of an artist's work is to stand in the presence of the artist. To make a connection, have an insight, to see the human, the person, flesh and blood accomplishment of the great work of art is truly something to behold. Do artists possess a more spiritual insight that is greater, smarter and more creative than someone who does not possess those same artistic abilities? I will leave that question for you to answer yourself.

26. Radii

In a scene we may only see parts of the circle or pyramid and may build on these parts through position or arrangement. Our imagination will fill in the blank space. The radii gives the feeling of attraction, diversion or expansion. It suggests a spirit of joyous movement such as a child at play extending his arms upward and outward.

This principle is illustrated in nature by the spreading of trunks of closely grouped trees, the spreading main branches of most trees, the petals of flowers and leaf arrangements that radiate from one point. The radii lines may be simple or complex, straight or curved. The center of interest should be near and centrally located in the frame. Variations of lines are important in adding interest to the picture.

Pictured at right, the bride's dress helps to build on the triangle implied by the slope directly adjacent to them. As the groom twirls the bride in a corkscrew like motion, it brings our vision down to the bottom left corner to finish this concept.

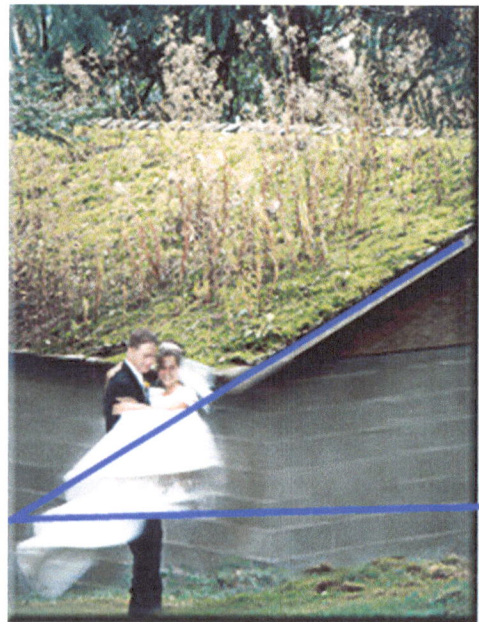

27. Rectangles

The rectangle or 'L' is a most useful and flexible composition. It suggests both dignity and repose. It is an attractive frame for all other forms.

Keep the 'L' composition simple and avoid too much detail. This can usually be accomplished by shooting from a low angle L-shaped landscape. Full-length portraits will appear majestic if the horizontal line is kept low in the frame. It is good to have a simple upright figure posed near the right or left side to give balance and interest to the picture. A picture with these qualities will be pleasing and restful in its simplicity.

The family at the bottom of the adjacent image is looking in different directions, which helps to strengthen the base of the photo.

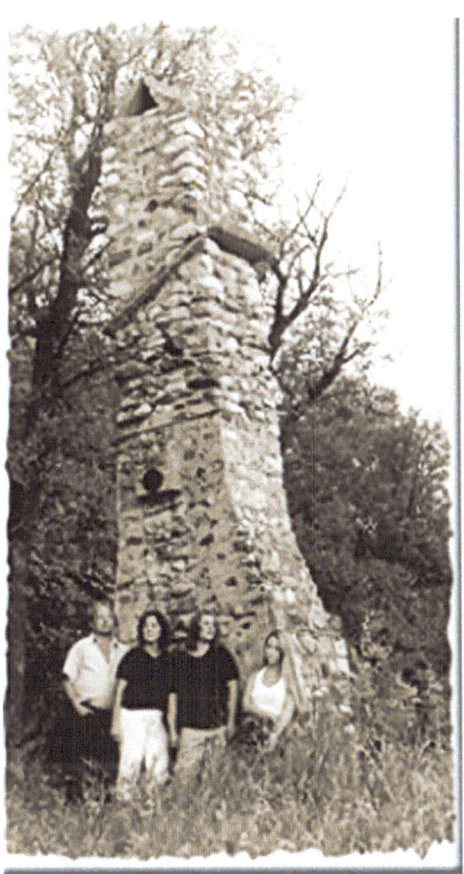

28. Planes

Look for many planes when shooting a scene in order to get a strong three-dimensional effect. A photograph with only two or three planes lacks depth and dimension. By "planes" we mean planes of material such as grass, soil, water, trees, sky, different surface texture, variations of land, light and shadows falling on a surface.

Pictures taken against the sun usually show more distant planes and better separation of subject matter. Shooting from a higher elevation can expand planes. A four-foot stepladder is most helpful. A high angle is usually better for most landscapes and general scenes. An added elevation of only three or four feet can make a marked difference in a picture by giving better plane separation and plane expansion.

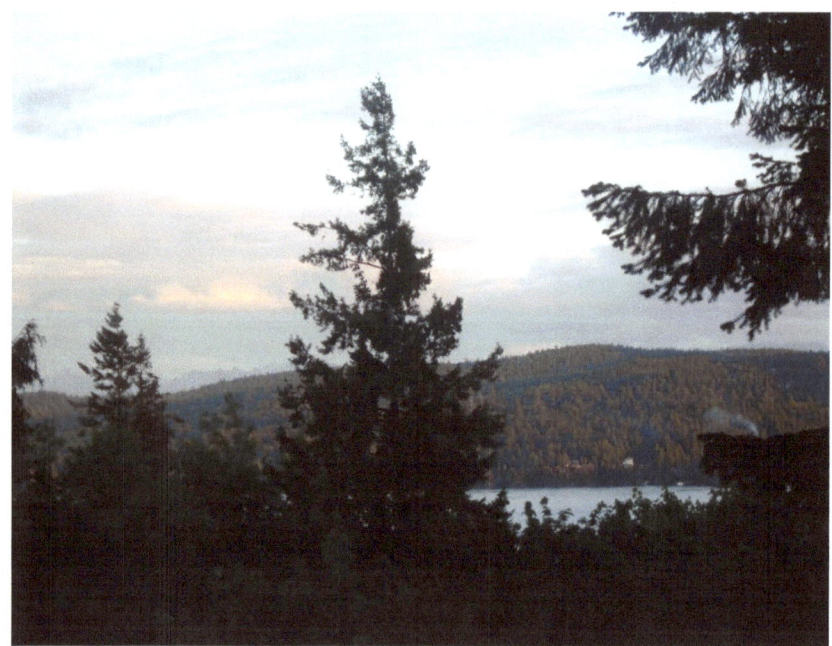

Photograph by Paul Rabinovitch

29. Colour Mergers

Colour mergers may blend the object with its surroundings. A natural way of protecting the animals and plants may be used to create patterns in our photography.

To compliment our portraiture, one may use similar coloured backgrounds to blend with the clothing an individual is wearing. The colour merger will give a slimming effect.

Another principle is controlling the illusion of depth. Lighting, overlapping of objects, perceptivism, sharpness of detail and tonal values are among these visual cues.

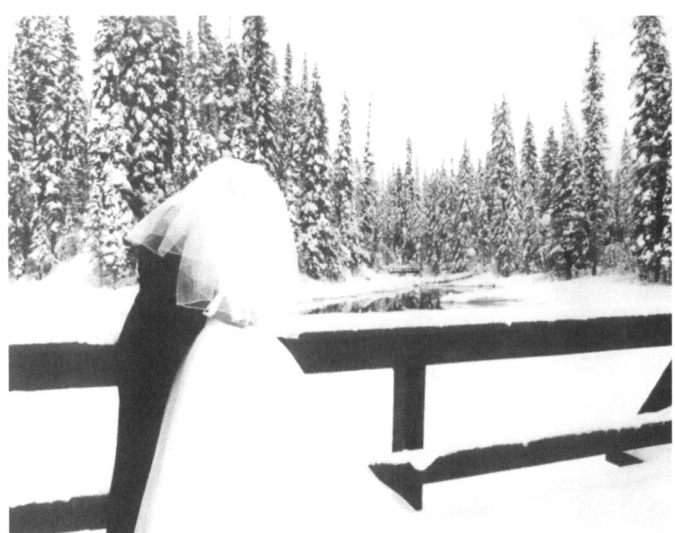

**Notice how the white of the
dress blends with the white of the snow.**

30. Perspective

The picture space you deal with has a peculiar property as it can be squeezed together or pulled apart. You can, with simple means which will be discussed later, compress photographic space so that things seem pushed together. Perspective, the familiar effect of closer things looking relatively larger than far away things, will be eliminated or weakened by this compression. On the other hand you can also expand space. This may be accomplished by making the apparent distance between objects much greater than normal, and causing nearby objects to loom disproportionately huge in relation to more distant ones.

Choice of shooting distance is important. If you move in very close to a foreground object, it will appear outlandishly big in comparison with more distant objects, and the distance between subjects and background will seem to be abnormally great. In a close-up portrait, a person's face might seem much larger than a house in the background. A right-angle turn is

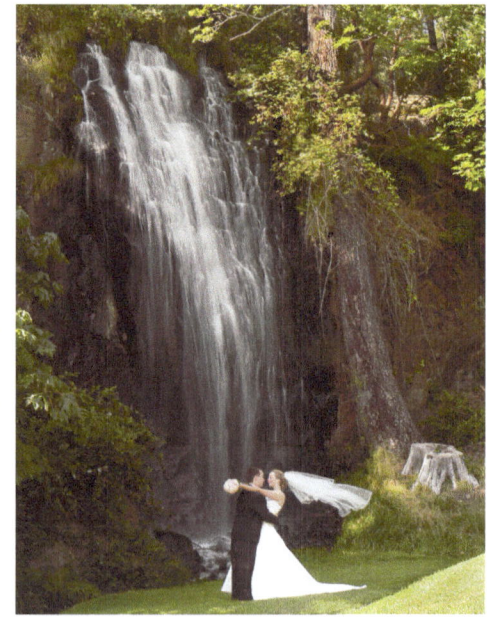

a useful photographic tool for this space-expanding effect. If you choose a distant camera viewpoint, one that is relatively far away from the nearest object, you will get the opposite effect. The same house will look large in comparison with the human subject. A long or telephoto lens helps you get this effect because it gives a large image of your subject even if you are a long way off.

In both these cases, it is not the wide angle or telephoto lens in itself that has any effect on depth and perspective. The lens makes it practical for you to shoot from a very close or very long camera position. Shooting distance rather than focal length controls photographic perspectiveness.

31. Exploration

Rarely, if ever, is the first view the best. Look at it from all sides, top and bottom. *Explore!* Search out the most dynamic angle because we have the opportunity to move the camera even if the subject is stationary.

If the camera is unmovable because of cramped space or if it is too impractical to move, then there are times when the subject can move. Explore by moving the subject. Sometimes perhaps if we are lucky, both the camera and the subject can be movable. This gives us a greater advantage to explore our subject in depth.

As was discussed in Principle 6, Separating the Subject and Background, this image is also very useful in revealing how a photographer can explore the space around them to capture a unique view. This image of the bride and groom at the piano was not originally envisioned in this manner. However, when climbing the stairs in the hotel and peering down at them I instinctively knew that this vantage point would provide a more appealing and dynamic angle from which to capture this loving couple on their special day.

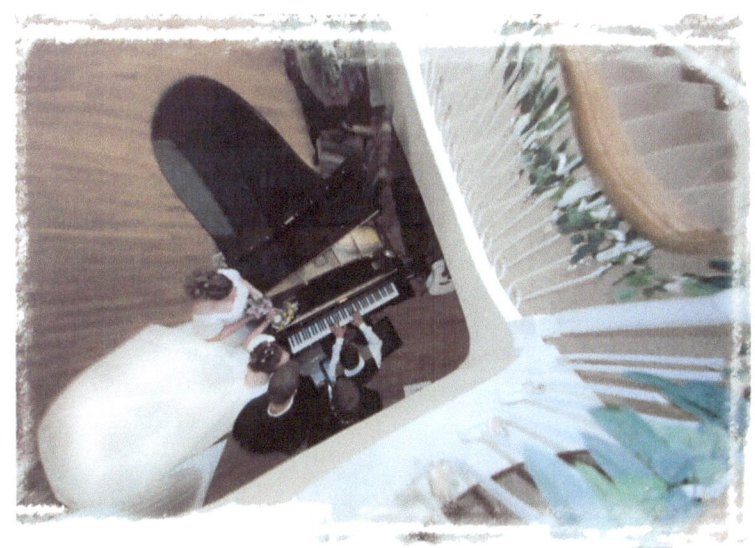

32. Isolation

The strongest way of seeing is always the most direct, the simplest and the most condensed. Separate the important from the superfluous by rearranging or removal to another place.

By filling the frame with the subject we can isolate the unimportant. Using a selective focus can blur out the unwanted foreground and background, thereby enabling the subject matter to stand out undistracted and isolated from the unimportant.

Another way of doing this is to use a high or low camera angle isolating the subject against an undistracting sky or uncluttered landscape background. In black and white we can use filters.

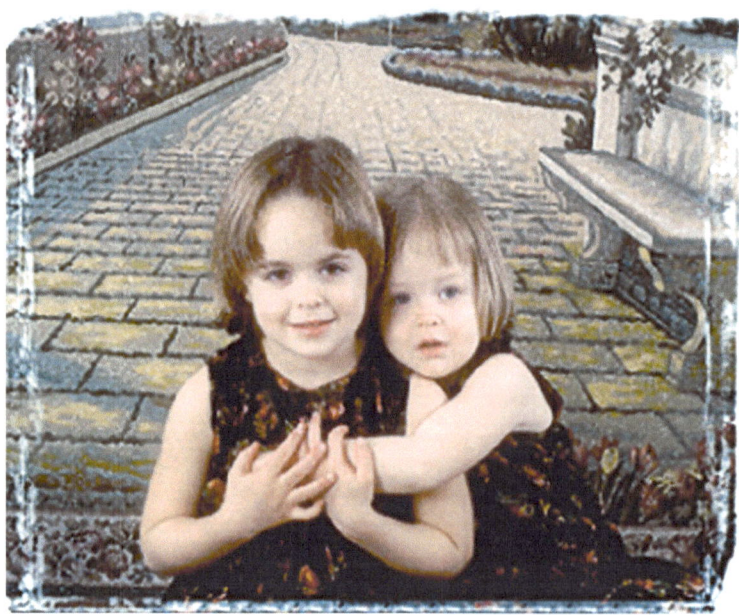

33. Organization

The essence of composition is organization. It implies order based on lines, forms, colours and relationships. In music, a beautiful chord gives pleasure to the ear in a harmonious manner. In a photograph, organization is harmonious and pleasing to the eye.

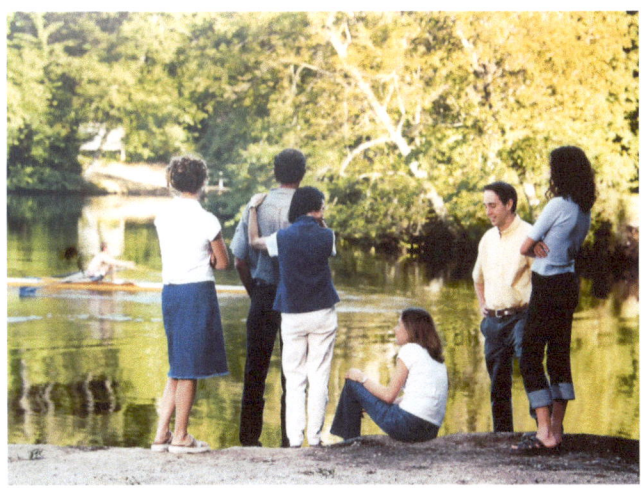

Comparatively, photography parallels music perhaps more than any other art form. Music is considered the universal language and in keeping, so is photography. Composers of music put together pieces that are played and replayed by others with a greater or lesser degree of skill.

In photography when a new composition has been seen, others of course will copy it with a greater or lesser degree of skill as well. As with music, fcw compositions are truly new. Emotions are expressed in and by music, and likewise the talented photographer displays feelings and evokes emotions from the viewer, be it love, hate, peace or disturbance.

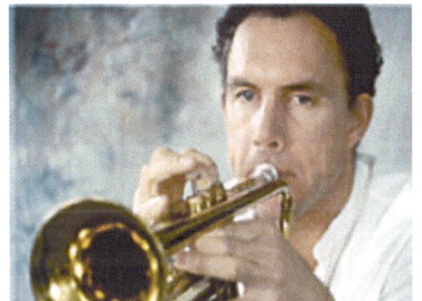

A mechanical instrument is employed in both these disciplines. The quality and intricacy of the equipment does not make the artist, although it may enhance the end result. A talented person may display their abilities even with the most primitive instrument.

In both music and photography, the untalented practitioner may learn to use the equipment to a limited degree. In all the arts we are stimulated in our minds depending on our experiences and sensitivity via our senses.

34. Perception

"Perception" in psychology is the act of being aware through one's senses i.e. seeing, hearing, tasting, smelling or feeling. As mentioned earlier, the importance need not always be shown, but the whole object is perceived from such parts as are present. Perception also means "observing."

The ability of the individual to perceive a series of fragments as the whole object depends upon many factors. Among these factors is the intelligence of the perceiving individual. Our background and training by concentrating on studies of perception may develop our skill in this area to a higher degree.

A group of elements in a complex situation are sometimes seen this way or that way. It is possible to discern several factors operating to make us perceive one particular possibility over another. The nearness of the elements to each other makes their perception parts of a pattern.

Elements that are alike tend to be perceived as belonging together. However, when elements are thrown together by chance, we seem to see familiar objects. When you see clouds against the sky, you see faces, animals or buildings, rather than just unfamiliar and meaningless figures. The pattern which "uses up" all the elements is the one which has the advantage in perception and its inclusiveness.

In part or in whole relationships, the parts of the relationship are perceived as belonging to the whole itself. What we see depends on surrounding conditions. The same set of lines may be seen as forming a block of wood. Their lines are physically the same, but their meaning depends upon the whole to which they belong. It seems that learning and past experience cannot explain this and other related phenomena.

Where interest is concerned, we see what we like to see. The principle of perception as outlined here and discussed in greater detail further on, is not absolute. Attach any interest to a pattern, and it will surely take over other combinations.

The shifting perception where the same object's situation may be observed in several ways is interesting. There is a quick automatic shifting in perception from one way to another. Reversible figures, however, are a slower shifting perception. This and ground illusions are exemplified through the example of a vase where we can see two faces.

How near or far something is can also affect our visual perception. The struggle for true perception mirrors the virtue of simplicity in relation to dominant elements and presenting them in basic forms and minimal tonal variations with harmony. This may be illustrated as a range of mountains, a vast body of water, or a desert scene. Perhaps the most outstanding characteristics of these are simplicity in pattern, simplicity in emotion, and simplicity in presentation.

An aerial view of the Rocky Mountains

Photograph by David Bohn

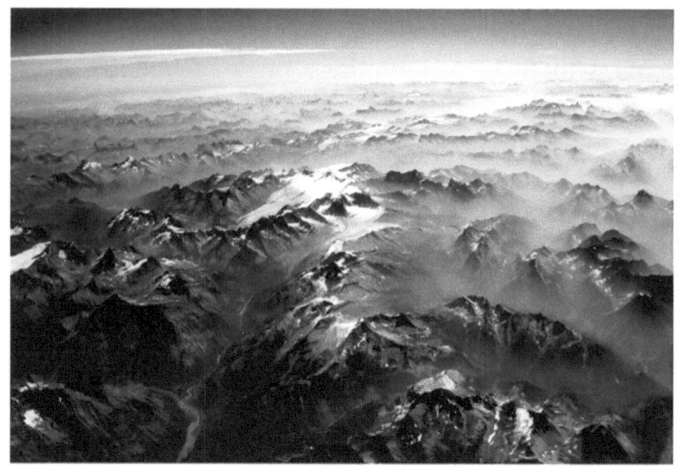

Another example is in the Imax movie "Magnificent Desolation: Walking on the Moon 3D" presented and narrated by Tom Hanks. There appeared to be a lack of perception when they came to the edge of a large valley. The viewer is unable to perceive it's mammoth depth. With this in mind, when composing our photographs we need to show that which is close to be larger than the objects that are far away.

35. Storytelling

Storytelling is as old as communication itself. A story is easier to remember and see in one's minds eye with a viewed imagination. We can alter and embellish the reality of the truth so as to make it more entertaining.

One example to illustrate this point is when my children were playing ball. David hit the ball in the air and Tammy tried to catch the ball but missed it and it hit her teeth. This is how the story was told to me, their father. I wanted to record this slice of truth as it was told to me. Tammy's emotion was dramatic and I loved David's sympathy and concern. Yes, that is what happened and it happened so fast that each retelling of the scenario kept changing. Therefore, by photographing the reenactment I was able to capture the truth as it stands today because memories tend to fade, change or are enhanced.

The memory of this event from childhood is now retrieved from the photograph because they may not have remembered the experience if it were not for the image in the photograph. Both David and Tammy now have to remember that day from what they are able to glean from the photo.

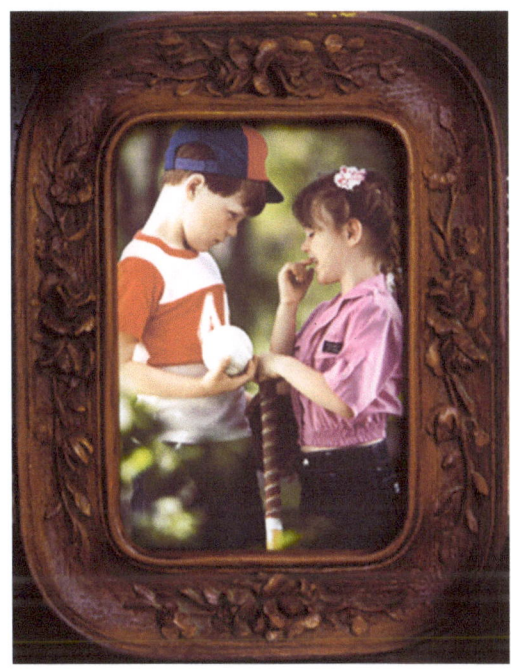

36. Pictures Have Edges

Pictures have edges, however our eyes are not hemmed in by any conscious boundary. Eyebrows and glasses form a frame of sorts, but these are so out of focus that we do not consider them and we are often not even consciously aware of them.

Our photograph has definite edges to consider. Through a camera, the area is cut down and compressed into a small rectangle or square with sharp corners and edges. These are artificial boundaries. Remember that hard edges and their height-to-width proportions have a very strong effect on the photograph. The image below illustrates this point in that even though a white background was used with the subjects wearing white shirts, the viewer's eyes still see the edges of their outlines as well as the sides of the photo that do not have borders or edges.

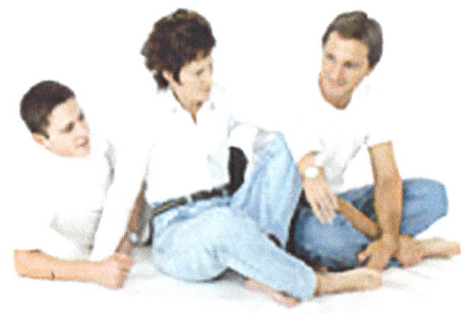

37. Monocular Vision

The camera has but one eye, which can also be described as monocular vision. Therefore, we should imply depth through converging lines, tones, shadows and different lighting techniques.

A good exercise is to cut out a rectangle or square shape and place it in front of your eyes. In so doing ensure that your peripheral vision is limited and that you are only left with a myopic view. Now walk around and discover how to see only as the format of the negative or digital file would represent the view to us.

Learn to see as the camera sees and not as our emotions would interpret. Normally we are constantly refocusing and looking elsewhere as our emotions are triggered. This is a good discipline to practice.

38. Discriminating Objects

The camera cannot select. We select what our eyes see by turning the head, focusing the eyes, and then the brain will generally disregard the unimportant parts. When talking to someone we are hardly aware of what is behind them. Remember the camera cannot discriminate other objects from the subject, and it usually records too much unwanted detail. You must try to narrow this down when planning your shot.

Discriminate is a harsh word today but we are forever choosing, eliminating and judging. Without this privilege we could not communicate effectively with impact and arresting vision. By selectively focusing and using an appropriate length of lens, we can help to eliminate and/or discriminate what is not wanted.

We have been afforded the responsibility to communicate the best we can. In so doing the viewer or reader can interpret not only what the photographer or author is saying, but also give the participant the benefit of the doubt that they may see more uniquely through their own experience and talent.

39. Movement

Movement has to be implied by the way that you position the subject within the photograph or by planning which part to blur. You may even allow the main subject to be blurred in order for us to show motion or movement. Then again, you could blur both the background and the subject as pictured here.

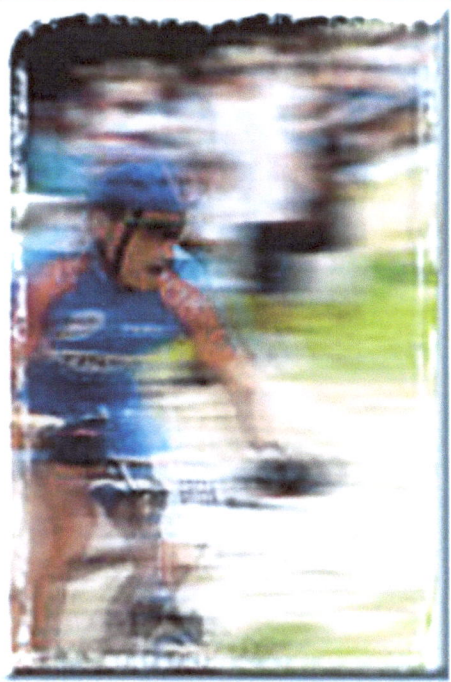

Roland Green
World Class Cyclist

40. Sequence

You can communicate a stronger, more elaborate story through a linked sequence. Photographing the action before, during and right after the main action has revealed its peak is effective. An example is World Class Cyclist Roland Green riding his bicycle during the race, his hands up in the air at the finish line and again on the podium accepting his award as pictured below.

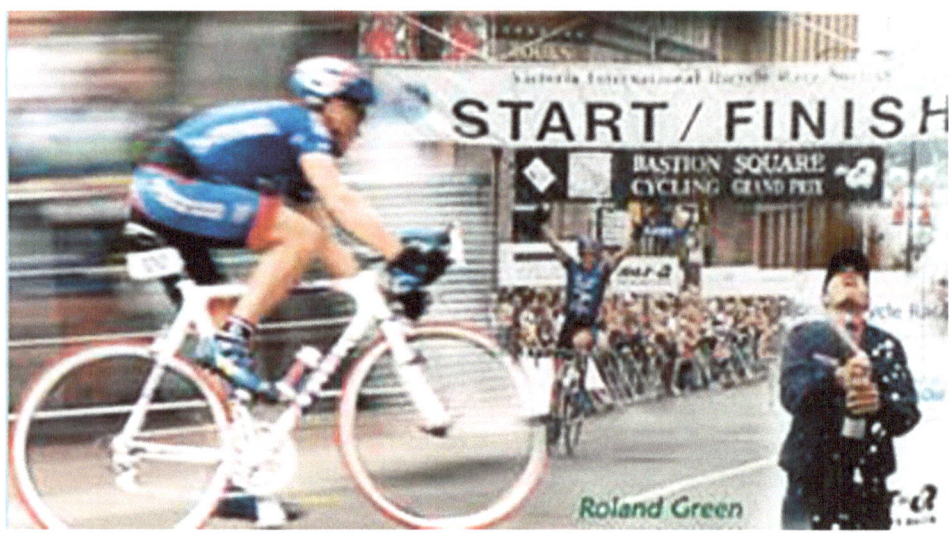

41. Tonal Interchange

Control the tone variations of light and dark. This will enable you to suggest depth, to emphasize important parts of the picture, compensate for colour and set the mood of your photograph. Differences in tone give separation. Thus setting the objects against opposite tones will provide more depth to the look of the picture. This technique is known as tonal interchange.

When photographing through a tunnel, the end of that tunnel is bright and the surroundings are dark. By placing a subject in the light at the end of the tunnel, the person will look dark and will stand out. Tonal interchange has created a different and an impressive effect.

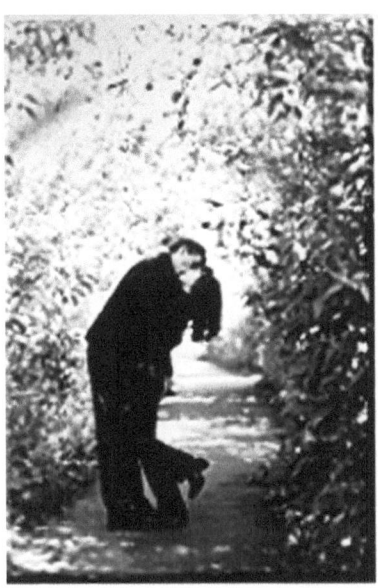

42. Reviewing Through Diagrams

Below and on the following pages are some diagrams to exemplify some of the principles that have been mentioned concerning composition.

A Low Horizon indicates increased space.

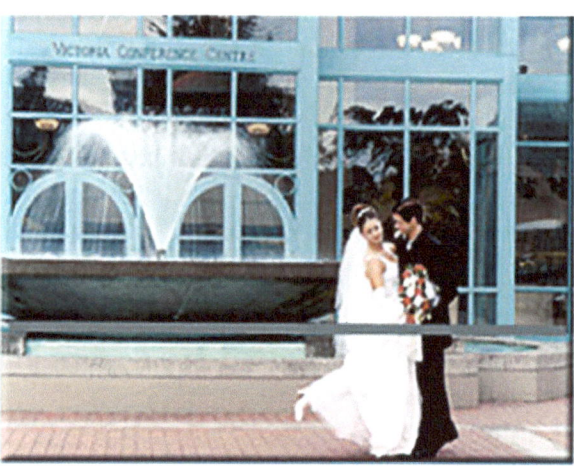

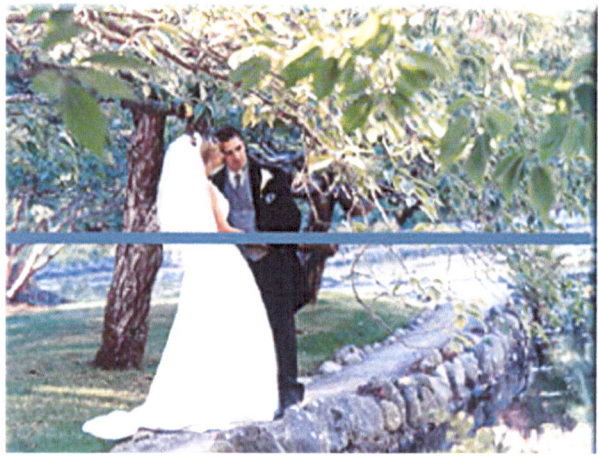

A Higher Horizon line tends to bring the background towards you.

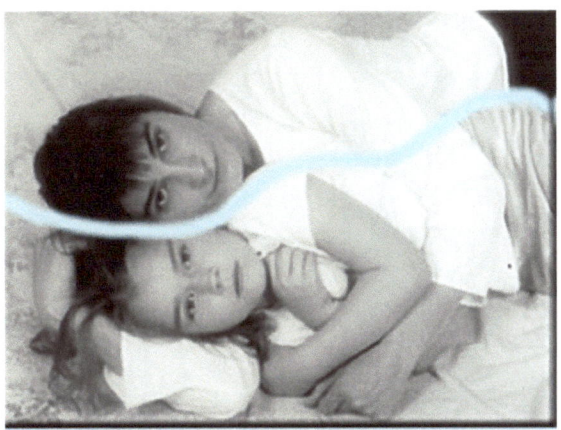

A rolling horizontal line
is a line of beauty.

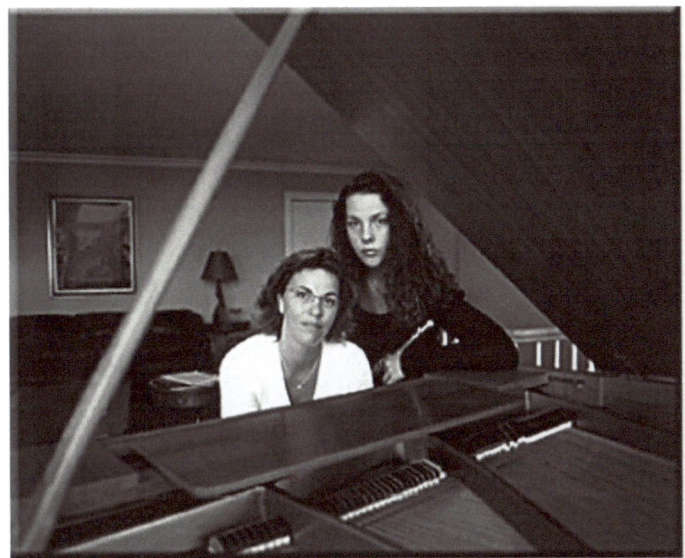

Triangles suggest
togetherness and attachment.

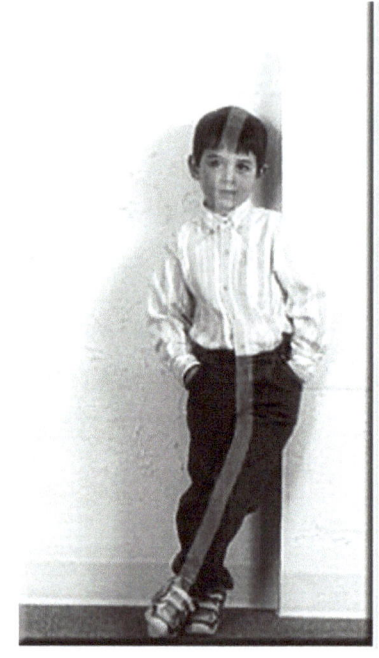

A directional "S" curve
exhibits a line under tension.

A diagonal line reveals action.

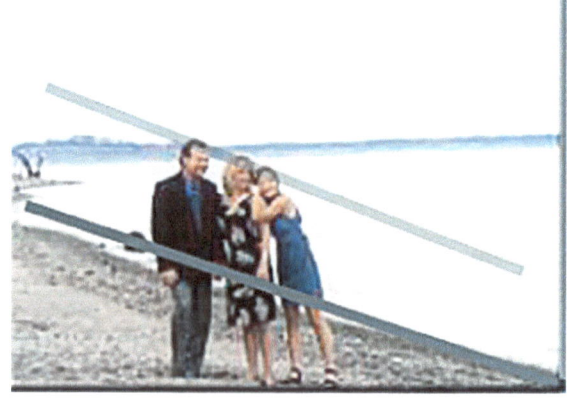

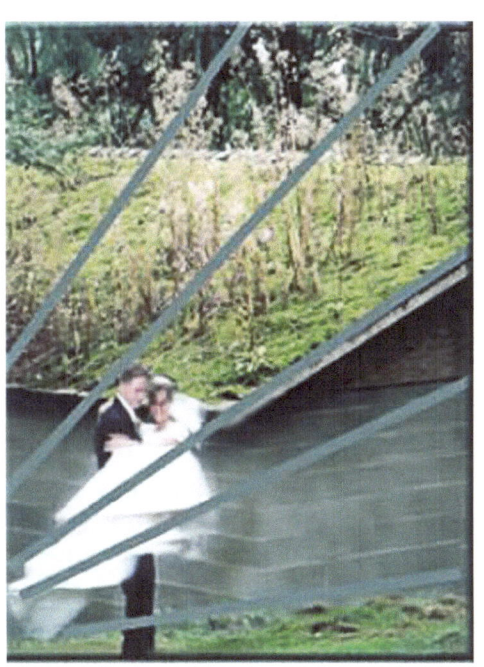

Sloping diagonal lines show movement.

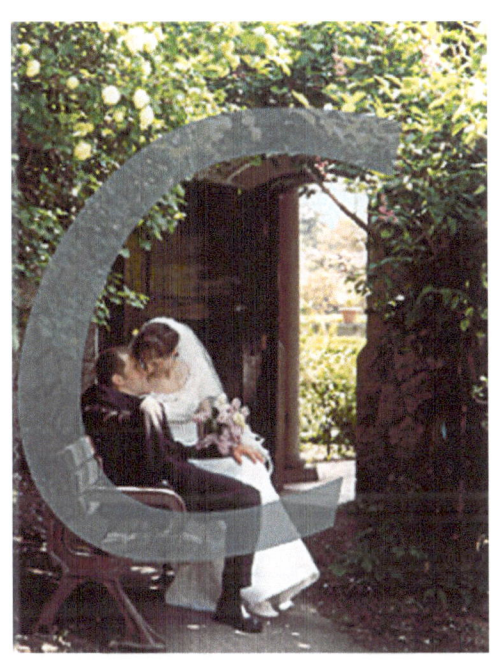

'C' shapes display a soft curve.

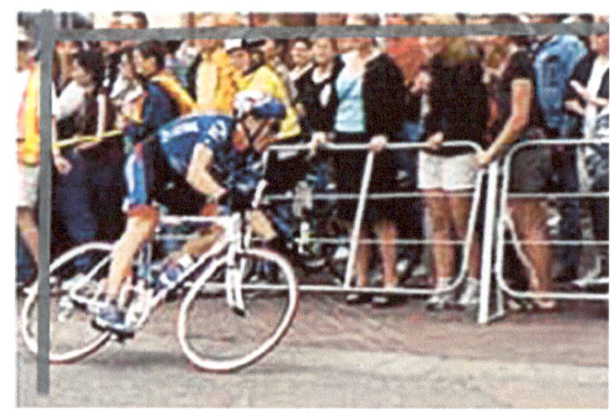

While an 'L' shape shows stability, as pictured in Principle 27, Rectangles, an inverted 'L' shape exhibits direction.

Other diagrams include the Thrusty "T" which discloses upward dominance, a Broken diagonal line that points out increased action, Horizontal versus Vertical lines, Positive versus Negative responses and Spatial depth.

43. Light and Texture

    The angle of light may increase the texture of an object. It may make it appear more or less rough depending upon the manner in which the angle of light strikes its subject.

    For example, when flying over a desert at high noon in an airplane, the desert may appear to be as flat as a table. However, at four or five in the afternoon when the light from the sun has dropped to about 45 degrees or less, the same desert may appear hilly and rugged. This is due to the highlights and deep shadows caused by a lower angle of light.

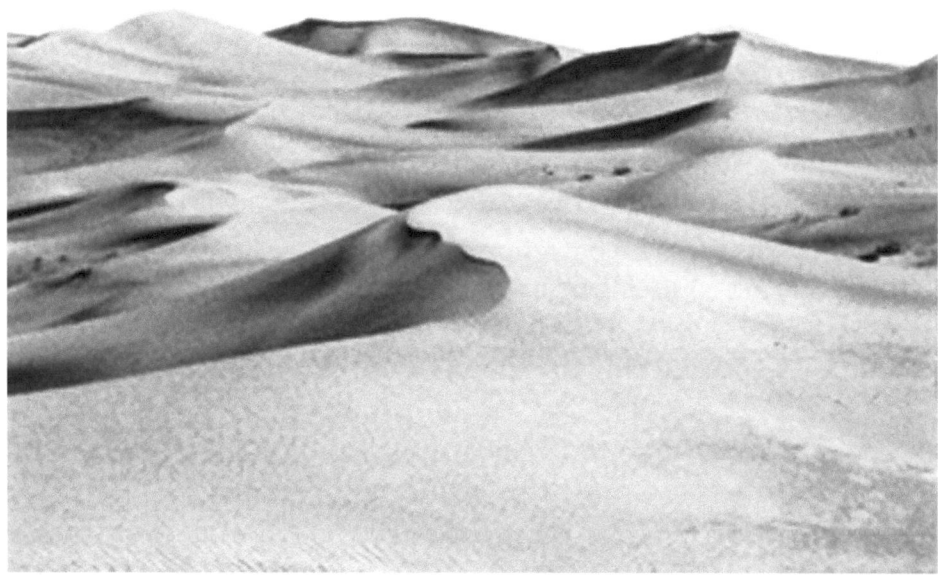

44. Time

Time embodies one of the basic properties of photography -- to capture a fleeting instant, a discreet slice of ongoing action. As in other arts, photography is dependent on the materials it uses. The recording of light is a property fundamental to the film, and the print and time create a function of controlling that light. Time and light are not mere tools of the trade, but important areas of concern for the photographer.

One way to read a picture can be to look at how the artist uses his materials. If one were to say that a painting is 'about' paint being applied to a surface, one would proceed to examine what kind is used and how it was applied. They could then make evaluations as to the quality and the effect that it has on the total image. Similarly, one can start looking at photography by saying that it concerns time, and one can explore how many ways 'time' is important to the photograph.

Photographers have become fascinated with time, both with the means to convey a scene of time, as well as with the subject of time itself as an abstract, philosophical concept. How does this fascinate the view? Partly, it presents a sense of reality in a way that the mind does not ordinarily perceive. Accustomed as we are to coping unconsciously with an endless flow of sensory perceptions, we stop to examine more closely something we feel we must have seen but yet never have, such as a motion frozen into a still image.

The classic illustration of frozen motion is the photograph of a galloping horse composed by E. Muybridge in 1878 entitled "Gaits of the Horse." Until the time of this photograph, no one had seen whether all four of a horse's hooves were airborne at the same time, and if so, what position they were in.

45. Symbol

A good photograph can evoke infinite associations from the viewer's own experience, other photographers and even the other arts. The symbol concentrates this function and creates new awareness. It is the result of the conscious or unconscious act of the photographer to imbue a detail, a gesture or a scene with a more universal meaning. With penetrating insight, one sees into the scene before us, and by using the appropriate symbol, arouses a corresponding intention in others. It gathers force as a continual calling forth makes it familiar and as each repetition evokes all accumulated connotations.

Symbolism has a wide range of uses. At one end of the spectrum a photograph presents an ordinary object or situation in such a way as to imply an enhanced meaning based on mutual knowledge of the object. At the other end of the spectrum, the views can be given a less specific scene. An equivalent such as a picture of just clouds where one is invited to be free, to associate and to investigate their own emotions and feed from the photographer's personal lexicon or dictionary of meanings.

46. Organizing the Picture

Numerous ways can be utilized to organize a photograph. Unlike a painter, the photographer has greater difficulty in building up the organization of the picture. The painter is more dependent on how he relates his image from a given chaotic environment, while a photographer can be appreciated for all the perception, balance of shapes, triangles, leading lines, etc. put into their image. A particularly relevant way to read photographs is to examine the way that "framing" was used.

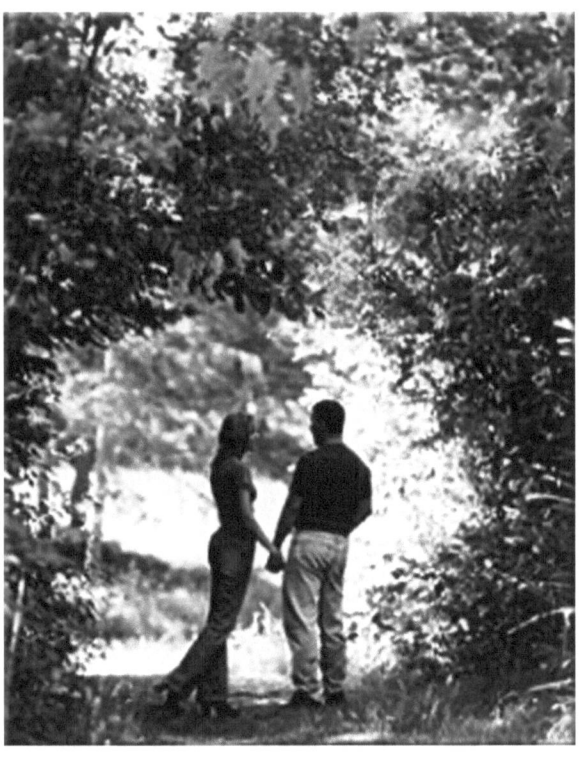

What is included or excluded from the picture becomes important as was previously discussed, and the placement of the center of interest to other objects by implication is happening outside the frame. The subject, for example, can be centrally placed in the picture, be contained and removed from the action of the world outside the frame. Thus set apart, its importance is enhanced.

A satisfying wholeness can present itself. Conversely, the photographer can work increasingly towards the edge of the frame, even using the edge to cut off objects. By partially or completely removing clues as to form, scale or position in a space, the viewer's ability to interpret the reality of the picture is frustrated. Ambiguity and tension is international. The eye is moved around the edge of the picture setting up a competing area of interest to the center. Likewise, the activity at the edge can draw the eye out of the photograph to imagine an action or form just outside the frame.

A "frame" can be placed within the picture itself, focusing attention on what is contained within it, as if it were a completely separate picture in its own right. What is within such an internal frame might very well be important to the content of the photo or if it is not, the mere fact that it is "framed" elevates it to an importance that the viewer feels they must justify. Similarly pictures have been organized like a diptych or triptych, 2 or 3 pictures hinged together, thereby creating a relationship between the panels, and offering an unexpected juxtaposition demanding a connection be made and telling a story metaphorically.

47. Abstraction and Ambiguity of Space

It is difficult to say why abstraction pleases the mind. Partially, it is the satisfaction of solving a puzzle and relating the abstract to the reality as we feel we know it. The schematic ordering of actuality meets the desire of the mind to see things whole and not in chaos.

In photography, the movement of the camera above or below normal eye level alters the way the subject appears on the film surface. Lenses flatten spatial relations into patterns on the two dimensional surfaces. The camera is placed so that key lines run into each other, destroying perspective clues and confusing identity of forms. The subject is framed so as to eliminate ready indications as to space and scale.

Ambiguity of spatial relations, as with ambiguity in content, attracts the mind like a magnet. It arouses curiosity and a desire to learn about the object. A tension is created between the accurate record one expects and the unexpected dimensions and relationships depicted.

What do you think you see in the image at right?

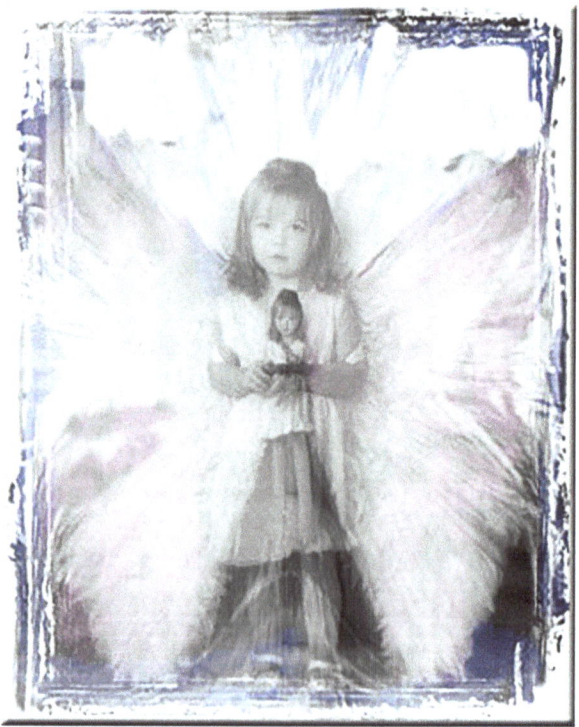

"Her Angel"

48. Surrealism

Almost all photographs contain surrealism to the extent that they contain some mystery or problems beyond reality to fascinate the viewer. The surrealist object is full of suggestion, and surrealism in photography is that which presents a wealth of innuendo, setting in motion an emotional response richer than the straight story confined by logical thought processes. The surrealist image is to be comprehended, not explained.

The photographs may deal with humour, nonsense, fascination, dreams, fantasy or an appeal to the subconscious and irrationality. This is a world where objects and ideas are not fully fashioned, but where images and our ideas of them are undergoing constant change, appearing and disappearing, or repeating with apparent accident.

Photographs in this mode shock and surprise in order to intensify experiences, destroy preconceived standards and evoke new impressions or ideas. They are more real than real, transcending the mere recording of reality! Even photography's facility for recording precisely and accurately can produce a clarity that is unreal or more surreal.

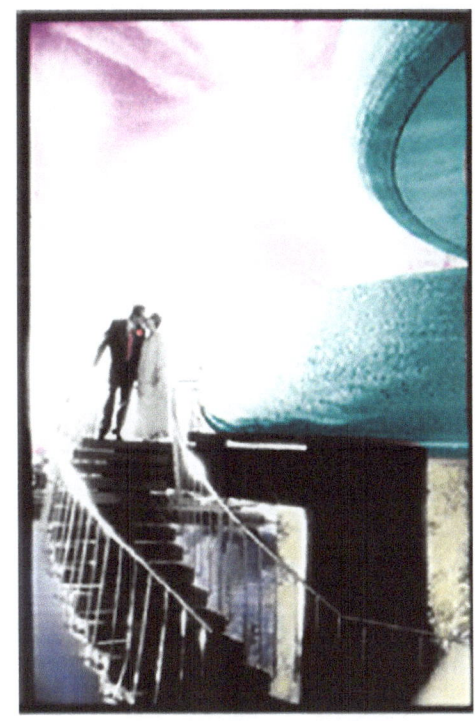

Infrared photograph

49. Light

Light is so essential to photography that it is no wonder that so little can be said about it in words. The eye itself is constantly reacting to light and is always startled to see the infinite changes and permutations that occur in everyday life.

Light reveals the unfamiliar and alters the familiar. It can make the ordinary unusual. Its patterns can create order or fragments; a whole can be created into new patterns. It evokes associations, moods and emotions.

Light can be the means of imbuing the subject with meaning, atmosphere, and poetic qualities, or light can be the subject per se to which the photograph addresses itself.

Raking across the surface of a building, light records its texture, volume and forms, intensifying the fierceness of its details. Light can also be graphic, reflecting areas of vision or creating patterns that cut across the subject matter of the photograph, super-imposing a second vision over the first. The converse of light is shadow, the abstract patterns made by light's absence. It reveals new, abstracted or distorted shapes, and provides punctuation to the text, thereby enhancing the rhythms of the image.

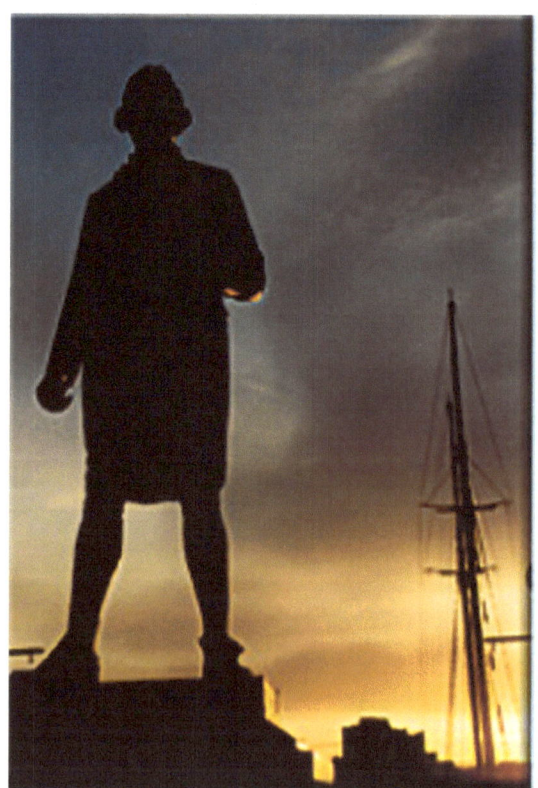

Photograph by David Bohn

50. Imagination

Normally in everyday experiences we are faced with five senses: taste, touch, smell, sight and hearing. In photography though, we are working under a handicap as four of the senses cannot be recorded. Non-visually we are compressing five senses into only one, which extremely limits our possibilities of expression.

We must funnel all our senses into our visual senses which is by no means an easy task. However when we begin in photography, we tend to greatly limit ourselves by omitting what we can use at hand ie. foreground, middle ground and background, in order to compose or put together a photograph that has in reality three grounds. Let's stop and consider these. We can use them to our advantage or disadvantage. Incorporate all three grounds in your photographs where possible.

We need to breathe life into our photographs. Imagination is our plus factor. We can imply certain things in a photograph through the use of imagination. We can imply the other four senses. In so doing, we will then sense reality in relationship to our past experiences. Think of a stove upon which is a frying pan that contains two eggs and several strips of bacon. Steam is rising from the pan and grease spits up as the bacon sizzles. Our imagination then fills in the missing senses.

Through our visual senses we can feel the heat from the stove, almost smell the frying eggs and bacon, and almost taste the food. In the back of our minds we can hear the crackling and sizzling of the food. Our imagination can then add the rest.

Imagination makes the image. One of our most important tools is imagination. By thinking out our photograph and then composing it accordingly, we will not restrict our imagination. Premeditating or thinking out each photograph before we put our camera in place is very important. Our finished product should have imagination. It should show feelings and personality and character!

Creativity in Photography

To produce a work which has the creative ability to reflect our understanding of photography, and not merely its mechanics, involves an understandable statement for the viewer.

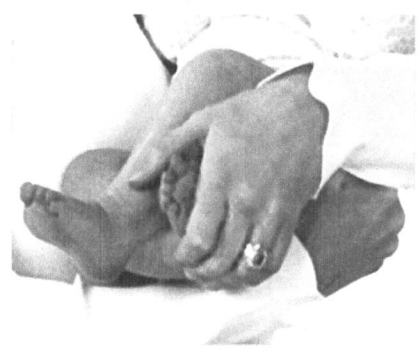

When examining this statement a little closer it can be overwhelming. An overview of photography from its historical beginning to the present reveals an ebb and flow in the genuine creativity in photography. The hit and miss snap shooting of today does nothing to promote photography as a distinctive art form. Education in photography's philosophy and historical influence, not merely knowledge of equipment, is required. To this end we need to be disciplined and dedicated with a consuming passion.

Having said the above, we need to first consider the elements in a more simplistic manner. First of all, most photographers have good or at least adequate equipment. This is presumed especially when we read of great men like Edward Weston (1886-1958) who created the Pepper #40 of which I have a student print. Weston is most famous for his natural forms, close-ups, nudes and landscapes. His creativity is remarkable not only because his camera was old and taped up which is a story his son told during a lecture in Calgary a number of years ago, but he also lived without running water, I believe, and yet had the drive, dedication and perseverance to pursue his art. He had what it takes to become more than a camera operator, he was truly one of the greatest photographers.

Let us look beyond the equipment, the chemistry and tools of the trade for now. Today, as opposed to the earlier days, we have the luxury of labs at our disposal. Is it really a luxury? Yes, I can say labs have been a good thing for the most part if we learn how to deal with them personally. I have valued the relationship with a few labs over the years, and even today I value my privilege to have one person at the lab look after my needs because they understand how I view my work. It is not a matter of getting the exposure just right or the colour just like the lab would prefer to make the printing easier. In reality nothing is perfect and if it is, it is artificial and not real. I need my work to have the human element visible. The only thing that is perfect is the imperfection of humanity.

I have always loved film but we need to graduate, or change with the times simply to keep up with the changing world. This does not make our work better, but perhaps just somewhat different. The digital process is in some ways more controllable if we have expertise in the use of a computer. I began with Radio Shack's model three, so you can see that I have been involved with computers for a very long time.

Control, control the negative, the chemistry, the enlarger. However now we must control the digital file on the computer and we, myself included, have in so many ways over done it that our work has become artificial. Arnold Newman, one of the world's most renowned portrait photographers, lectured in Victoria, British Columbia, a number of years ago and started with this opening statement, "All those photographs awarded as winners are so artificial..." Some of my favourite images are not perfect. I was judging a National competition one year and fought for an image that didn't follow the rules. I remember this well as Hugo Redivo, a well respected Master Photographer in his own right, and I were in complete agreement.

"All portraits are accurate, but none are the truth."
~Richard Avedon

It is important to keep abreast with the changing times, but it is equally important to not forget that you can produce good images and may even stand out from the crowd when we apply our ability to our craft. In so doing, we become craftsmen and there is nothing wrong with being a craftsman. A craftsman has the ability to stick with a job and produce images that are refined and perfectly polished. Is it art? You be the judge.

There are always a few who have a special gift. It is born in them and cannot be taught. It just is and there is no way of explaining this talent. A person with the drive to succeed will find a way to overcome the everyday stresses of life. Just think of Vincent van Gogh (1853-1890). Here is a driven man. He took drugs to keep his sanity and yet his work was unappreciated for many years. While he was able to quit his life, he was unable to quit his art!

Photography

What is photography? This is a serious question and one that is not as superficial as we might think!

We know in part, at least, the mechanical features of the camera body and to some extent the optical assembly. We might not be completely ignorant about film processing in regard to words or the film's tolerance. We have done the paper process known as enlarging to the amateur at least in a black and white work. Do *we* understand photography?

Our subject, our imagination, the type of film paper, lighting and the environment should all be part of the photographic process in our mind before the button is pushed. What about the viewer? The public?

If photography is the universal language then it must be clear. Absolutely clear to everyone, all cultures, all levels of education and beliefs, even though the public's views may differ depending on their perception and background.

When we look at a photograph as a viewer, how are we exercised? Is our imagination filling our senses? Normally everyday experiences are faced with our five senses. In photography we are working under a handicap. Four of our five senses cannot be recorded. Non-visual, we are compressing five senses into only one, which extremely limits our expressions. We must funnel all our senses into only one, our visual sense, which by no means is an easy task. To breathe life into our photos, imagination is our plus factor.

The Driven Man

They all say, your young life is before you;
I know it is short, with so much to do.

They call it a job: it's a living;
I know it is the purpose for life.

They call it relaxation, rest, enjoyment;
I know it is laziness, timidity and self-indulgence.

They all say you owe it to yourself;
I know it is human nature: it craves attention.

They call it fanaticism;
I know it is future growth.

They all say live for the present;
I know it is the future that holds the goal.

They call it sacrifice;
I know it is a labour of love.

We need to be like a nail, willing to be driven for the sake of supporting photography. Someone who will not bend to the pressure of our media and society. Nailing together our present and our past.

- Klaus Bohn

Closing Remarks: A Summary

It would be less than honest to say that the 50 principles are all there is to composition. These principles are only a starting point, briefly explained to whet the appetite of an interested student of photography.

The explanations of each principle were kept short by intentional design so that the reader may give thought to, and relate to each one with respect to their own personal experiences and tastes. It is hoped that each person will, on their own, expand these principles in their life through further reading and the experimentation process.

A photographer has but one right… to be a continual student!

With the above thought in mind, I would like to suggest a little homework. A few years ago when I was teaching a visual class, one project I provided was that the students photograph the alphabet in natural design. I had 12 students and one finished the project in record time. It was quite remarkable how she was able to find all the ABC's in nature.

Please consider this task as it will improve your visual acumen. This project is harder than you might think. You will learn to *see* like never before. There will be images in all you see, and the "aha" factor will kick in and you will be glad you did it!

Give it a try!

About the Author

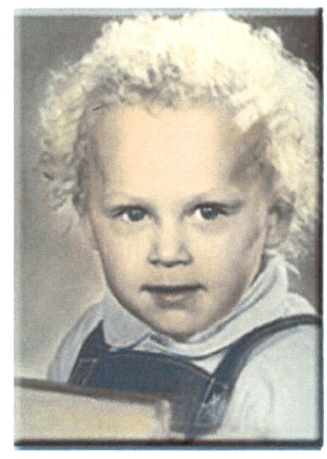

Klaus Bohn was born in Germany shortly after World War II, and came to Canada as a small child with his parents and settled in Saskatchewan. He enjoyed art in school, especially drawing. A few years after graduation while on holiday in Europe, his two friends with 35mm cameras had a desire for superior composition which left its mark on Klaus and what has turned into a lifelong journey.

In 1972 he graduated from the Winnona School of Photography and over the years has attended private classes from well known photographers who have lectured throughout the world including Joe Zeltzman, Monte Zucker, Linda Lapp-Murray, Donald Jack, Rocky Gunn, Yousuf Karsh, Arnold Newman, and many more.

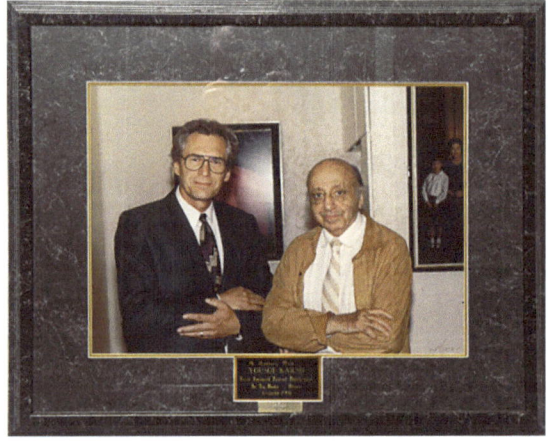

Klaus Bohn & Yousuf Karsh
Photograph by Mitch Hippsley

Klaus started to work for a studio in Saskatoon in 1974 and then opened his own studio in Moose Jaw, Saskatchewan in August of 1975. In 1978 Klaus was commissioned to photograph Her Majesty, Queen Elizabeth II during her Royal visit to Canada.

A few other notable people who Klaus has photographed over the years include: Grammy Award winning singer Anne Murray, world-renowned best selling author Norman Vincent Peale, Emmy Award winning actor, best selling author and successful businessman Art Linkletter, former Canadian Prime Minister Brian Mulroney, best selling author of the "Chicken Soup for the Soul" books Mark Victor Hansen, NHL Hockey All-Star of the Calgary Flames Theoren Fleury and World Class cyclist Roland Green.

Over the years he has worked to develop his unique style and received his Fellowship (F/SPPA) and Craftsman (CPA) in 1987 and his Masters of Photographic Arts (MPA) in 1989. He has also received his Accreditation in Child Photography along with many other awards for Excellence in Photography. To the best of our knowledge, Klaus was the first photographer to ever hang a "bromoil" print.

He has been an active executive member of the Saskatchewan Professional Photographer's Association and held the title of Education Chairman as well as other positions. Klaus has also been a member of the Professional Photographers Association of British Columbia, Professional Photographers of Canada, the Professional Photographers of America and the Royal Society of Great Britain.

Klaus has taught professional photography since 1984 across Canada and the United States. He was invited to speak at the National Photography Convention in Las Vegas. Klaus has also lectured to camera clubs including the Canadian Camera Club's National Convention as well as other community organizations. Always trying to assist amateur and professional photographers alike, Klaus has also judged at many National and Regional photography competitions.

He has authored several magazine articles published in Range Finder Magazine, the Professional Photographers of Canada (PPOC) Magazine, as well as a series for the Briar Patch Magazine. Many of his photographs have been published including several magazine covers. Klaus has also been published in several books including, "Wedding Portrait Photography World" by Jack Curtis, "The Practice of Modern Photography" by D. H. Moore, and "Promoting Portraits" by Paul Castle.

Presently residing in Victoria, British Columbia, Klaus owns his own studio business, "Photographic Art." His current endeavours include writing and exploring new unique forms of photographic art including watercolours and bromoil prints. Klaus' upcoming projects include a book on portrait photography that will reveal in great detail other unique aspects of composition that are specific to portraiture. These insights, gained from decades of discovery, will be shared to assist all photographers capture more creative and vibrant images. You too will be "Feeling more deeply about photography."

<u>Photographic Watercolour & Bromoil Print Examples</u>

Here are some examples of photographic watercolours Klaus has produced recently.

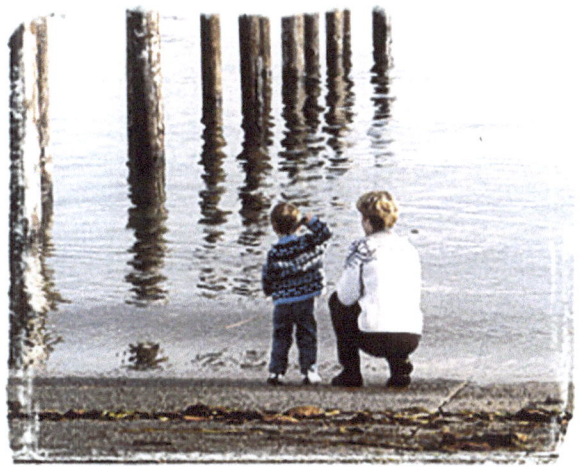

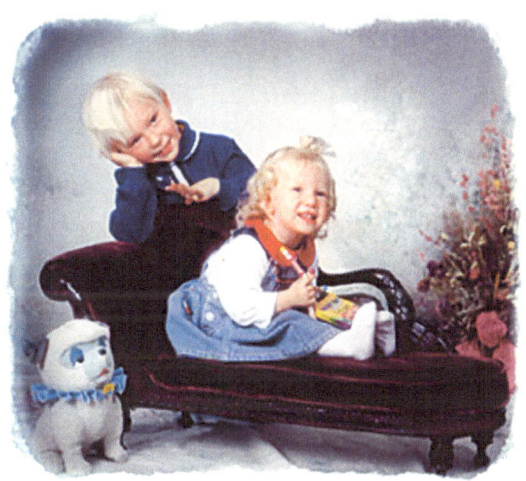

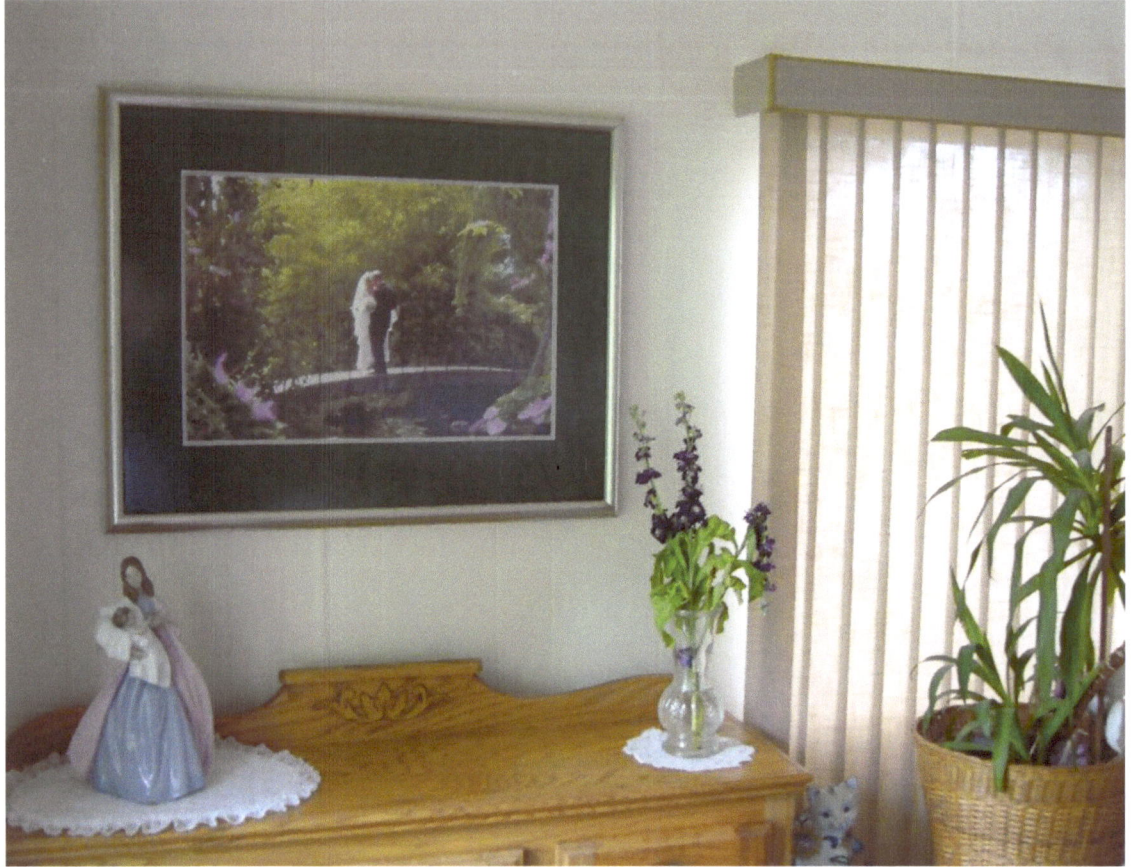

Photographed by Paul Rabinovitch
Photographic Watercolour inset by Klaus Bohn

As I once wrote in an article that appeared in the Professional Photographers of Canada (PPOC) Magazine, "From the beginning of photography everyone has been impressed with their image on a wall. Unlike photography, everyone has not changed in this respect."

When photographing a wedding, the couple is encouraged to see beyond the standard album and 8 by 10 inch framed prints. By offering photographic watercolours these images then become works of art proudly displayed in the couple's home. The images used for these photographic watercolours are not the standard formal shot often taken at weddings. Instead, an intimate portrait of the couple is envisioned by understanding the client's desires and needs.

In the image above, this loving couple wanted to capture the special intimacy they experienced on their first date in which they strolled through Beacon Hill Park in Victoria, British Columbia. This was of particular importance to the bride as she had tossed a coin into the water and made a wish, "To someday marry this man." Having stayed in touch with this couple since their marriage, they often tell me how they cherish this special remembrance of that day. This couple proudly displays this keepsake in their home.

Should you wish to consider creating photographic artwork, you would be wise to follow the advice of D. H. Moore in which he said, "…the frame must always be visually subordinated to the photographic image!" Always remember that you are only limited by your creativity and imagination when exploring the world of photography.

My drive has always been to learn alternative processes. When I heard about the bromoil print process in 1994 I became quite intrigued. World renowned photographer David W. Lewis set up a class for two of us and we flew out to spend a few days with David in Ontario. It is one of the most difficult processes, but it has a rich reward in learning to master the process.

We began by making our own paper, while I believe David used paper that he had purchased from France. The steps we learned took my breath away. The chemistry, inks, oil, brushes from England, putty knives, paper, chammy, and so much more.

We were then instructed on how to expose the paper 25%, 50%, 100%, 150%, 200%, over or under, depending on the negative contrast density. Once we have this dialed in then the matrix had to dry until the next day. The next step was to super heat the matrix and start to ink the paper. This is the most difficult part, layer after layer, and the more layers the more beautiful the images become.

The process is quite complex, but suffice it to say that as you can imagine there is so much more to the bromoil process than is discussed here. I love the art of it, the longevity of it, the difficulty of it, and the beauty of it. It produces an image that could not be produced in any other way. The photographers of old truly were craftsmen and dedicated their lives to their craft without sufficient compensation, yet had the drive to do so.

David W. Lewis is still teaching bromoil classes. More information may be obtained at David's web site: **www.bromoil.com**. I would highly recommend these classes if you want to stretch your own personal learning curve.

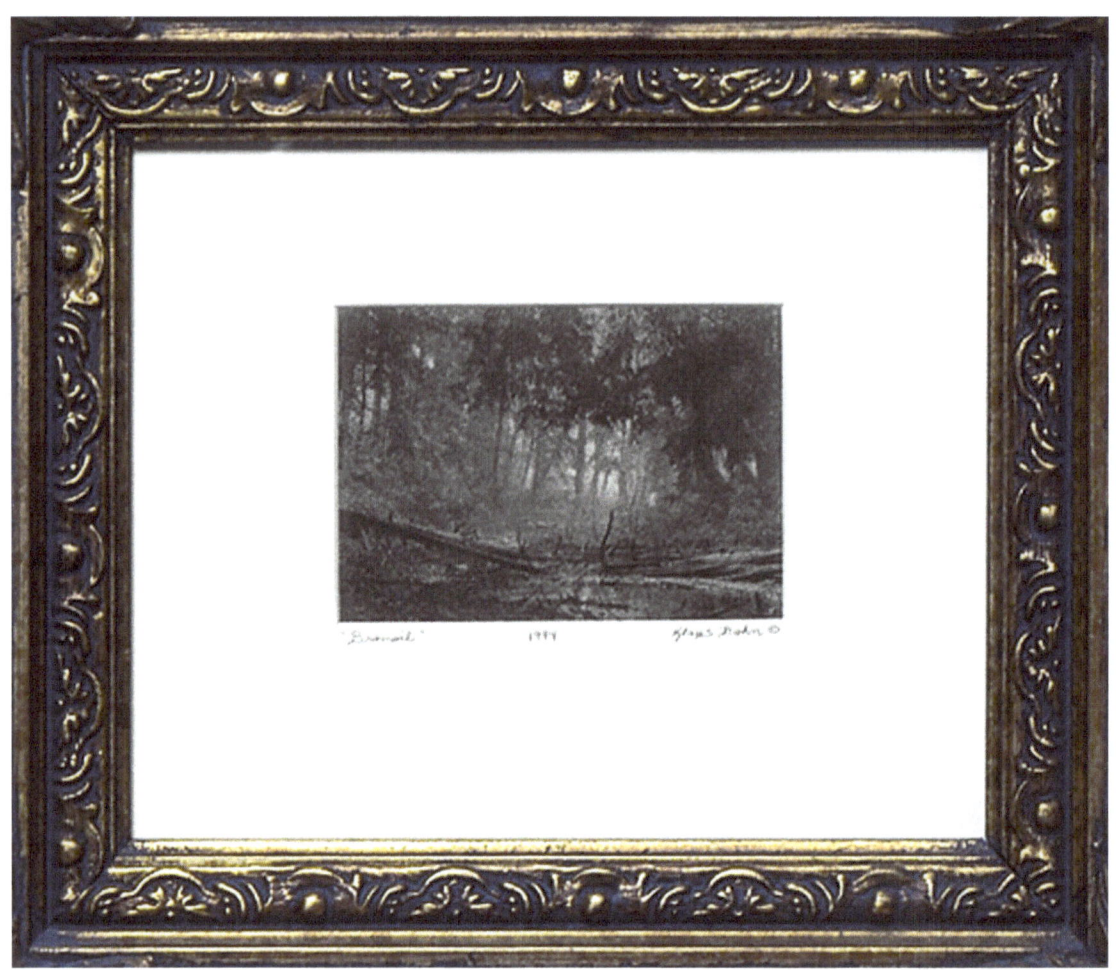

Logs in the Forest

On the opposite page is a photo of my very first bromoil print that I completed in 1994. The image depicts fallen logs in the forest. This bromoil is most precious not because I didn't take the photo, but that I made it into a bromoil. I oiled the paper and it turned out so well for my first attempt at this difficult process.

I had the possibility to sell the image a number of times but it is like my first born, my baby. I couldn't believe it as I applied layer upon layer, many layers, and I had seemingly the soft touch that is necessary for the making of bromoils.

The depth is so evident because of layering the ink, the softer the touch the more delicate and depth there appears in the image. A viewer can see right to the light through the trees. The fallen logs in the foreground prevents the eye from racing through the picture, holding one back for a few split seconds as we journey deeper into the photograph. The haze like feeling brings back memory of early daytime when the air is fresh and the dampness of the dew hovers as it were for its given time.

Something so woody and large in scale can feel so delicate and soft to touch us not only visibly but also emotionally.

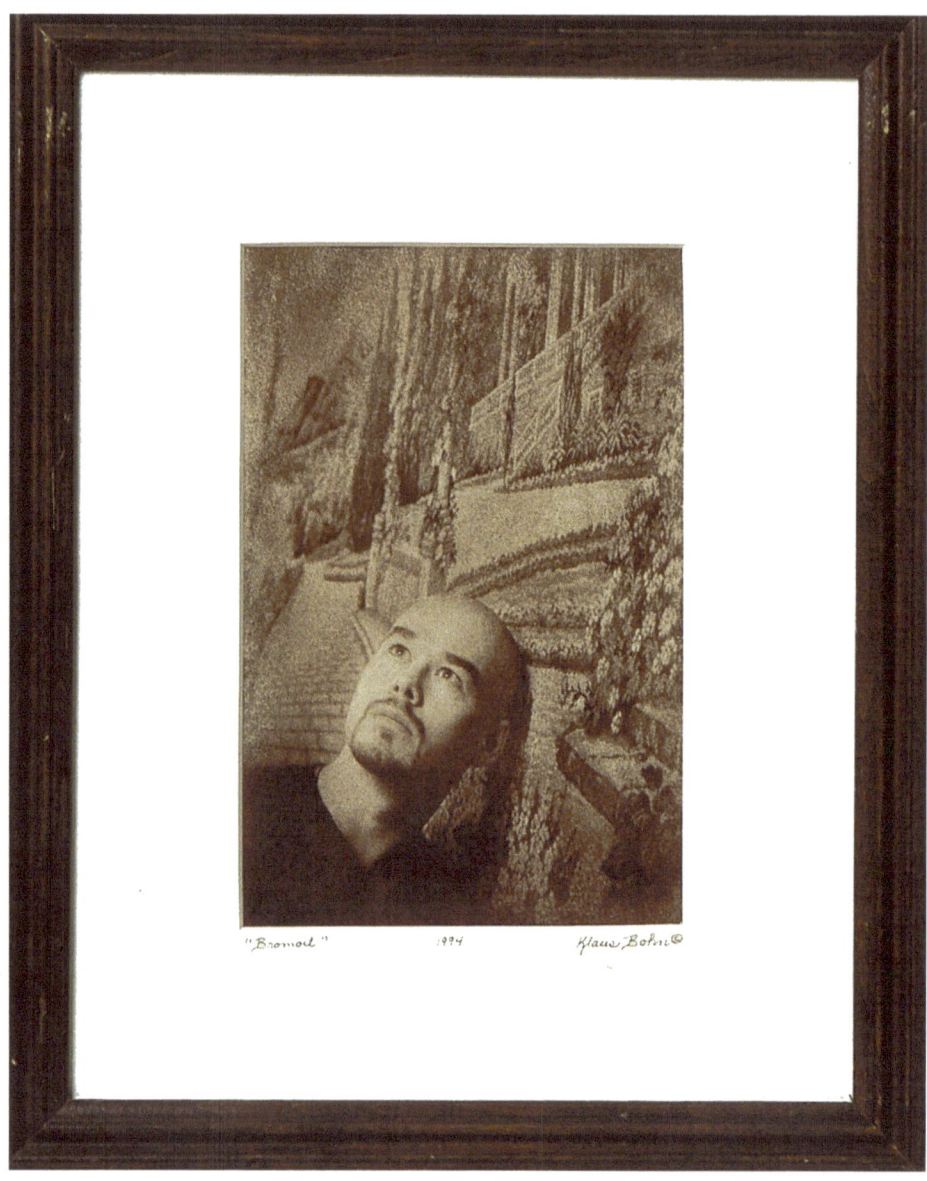

"Bromoil"   1994   Klaus Bohn ©

Portrait of a Man

When this man came into my studio I felt a connection some how, and yet I didn't know him when he said, "I need something, an image of myself because I'm a director for plays at a very large school. I would like it to fantasize my dream, the work I'm doing NOW."

Most people want a clear cut image of reality. They will often say, "Wow, that is a sharp picture… your equipment is expensive and that is why your pictures are sharp." Of course that is not why. I sometimes, more often than not, like the image to be soft and exude a feeling.

My feelings were a representation of this bromoil as it needed to be thoughtful, dreamy, insightful and have the possibility for this young director to grow. The path he has already travelled by learning from the past, from the greats and moving up and forward, there can be no other direction for this director especially as I got to know him. I love to work with creative professionals because they step back and give themselves to the artist.

The tapestry speaks to me of the history of directors going back to the ancient days of the European culture and Shakespearian influence. With the man at the bottom looking up it gives us a feeling of possibility, growth and longevity. His thoughtfulness gives me a feeling of creativity and this young man has just that.

I was impressed by him, profoundly so.

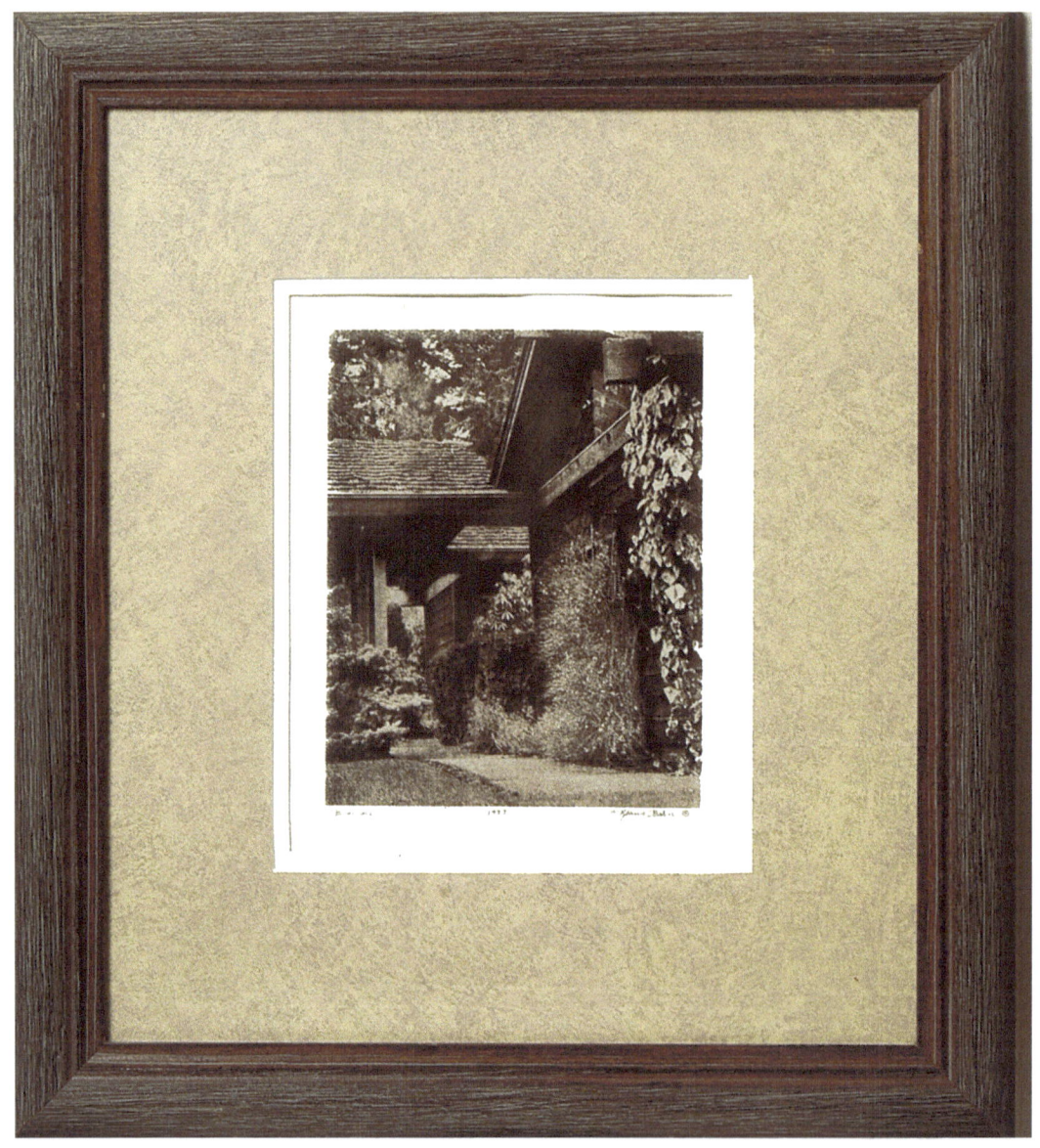

House in Victoria

I looked at this house a number of years ago and entertained the thought of purchasing it, and perhaps I should have, I know I should have, there was so much I liked about the house. Without going into detail, let's say it held me captive long enough to photograph it and produce a bromoil.

Maybe the sentimental value only excites my mind because of how I felt at that time to move to Victoria, such a peaceful and serene place. I needed that at that time even more than I knew, in retrospect.

I like the way the house was nestled into the trees almost like being on a private acreage. Prior to moving to Victoria, we were living on a 127-acre property in Saskatchewan. Of course this was nothing like that, but it felt private and comfortable.

The angles and shapes of the house felt artistic and the swimming pool inside looked inviting, the possibility to live within, without going anywhere for a long period of time. I have always been a private person at heart. People think they know me but are mistaken.

Very few know me, really know me and that is very much ok with me, ok by design!

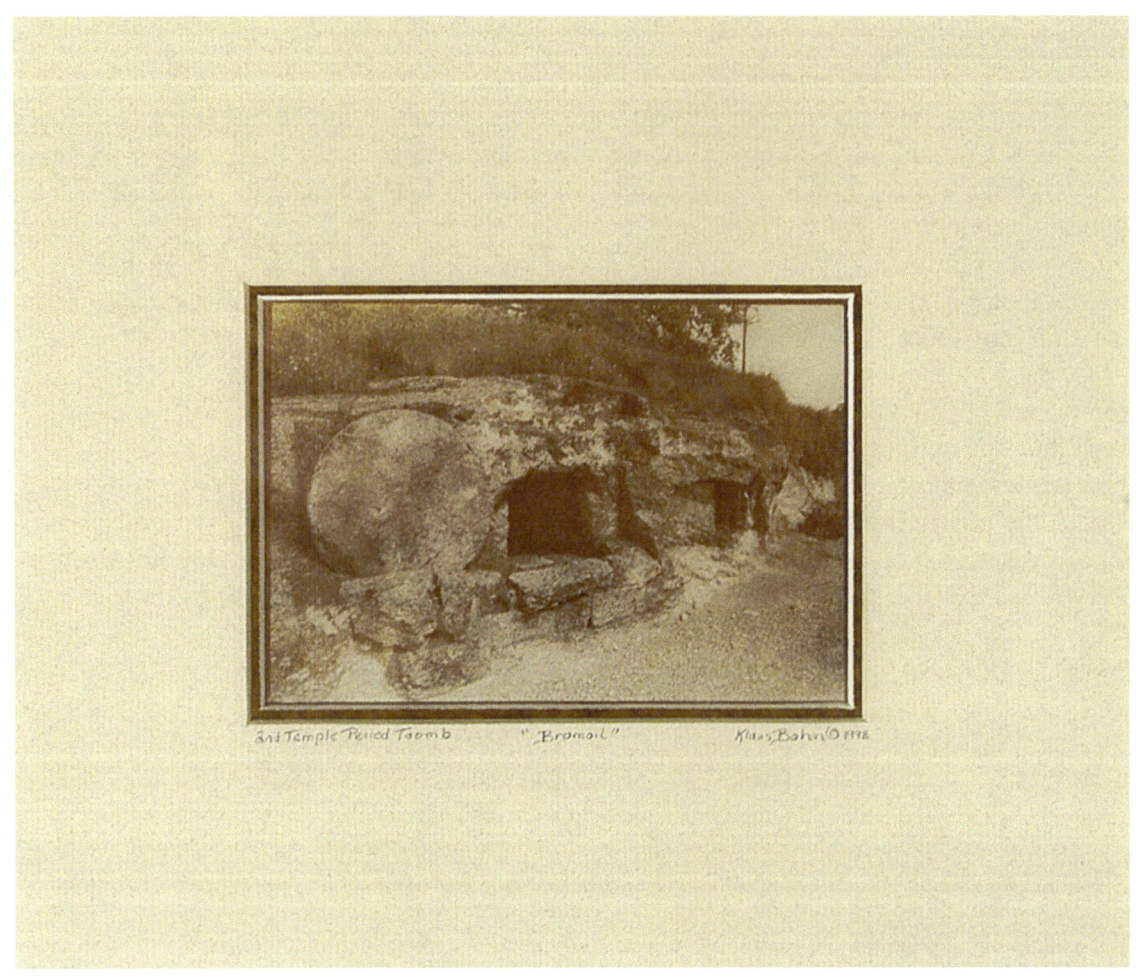

2nd Temple Peiied Toomb   "Bromoil"   Klaus Bohn © 1998

2nd Temple Period Tomb

In 1998 I photographed this 2nd Temple Period Tomb and made a bromoil in the same year. As we were travelling down the road in a tour bus I yelled, "Stop the bus I need to photograph that tomb!" The tour guide said, "We can't stop on this road," but I pleaded with her and the bus driver gave in and said that I was the only one allowed out but only for 10 seconds. Yes I took only a few seconds, believe you me, they mean what they say especially the military.

To see and witness an old grave site at least a century or no doubt much older was incredible. The tour guide didn't know, she said perhaps two centuries, but all this is guess work. A century more or less doesn't seem to matter in very old countries.

I was in awe of the dates of things, even very old buildings, grave sites, etc. This grave site with the large rolling stone still there preserved for us to see and try to imagine what it would have been like so many years ago.

Making it into a bromoil paid homage to this almost unimaginable sight.

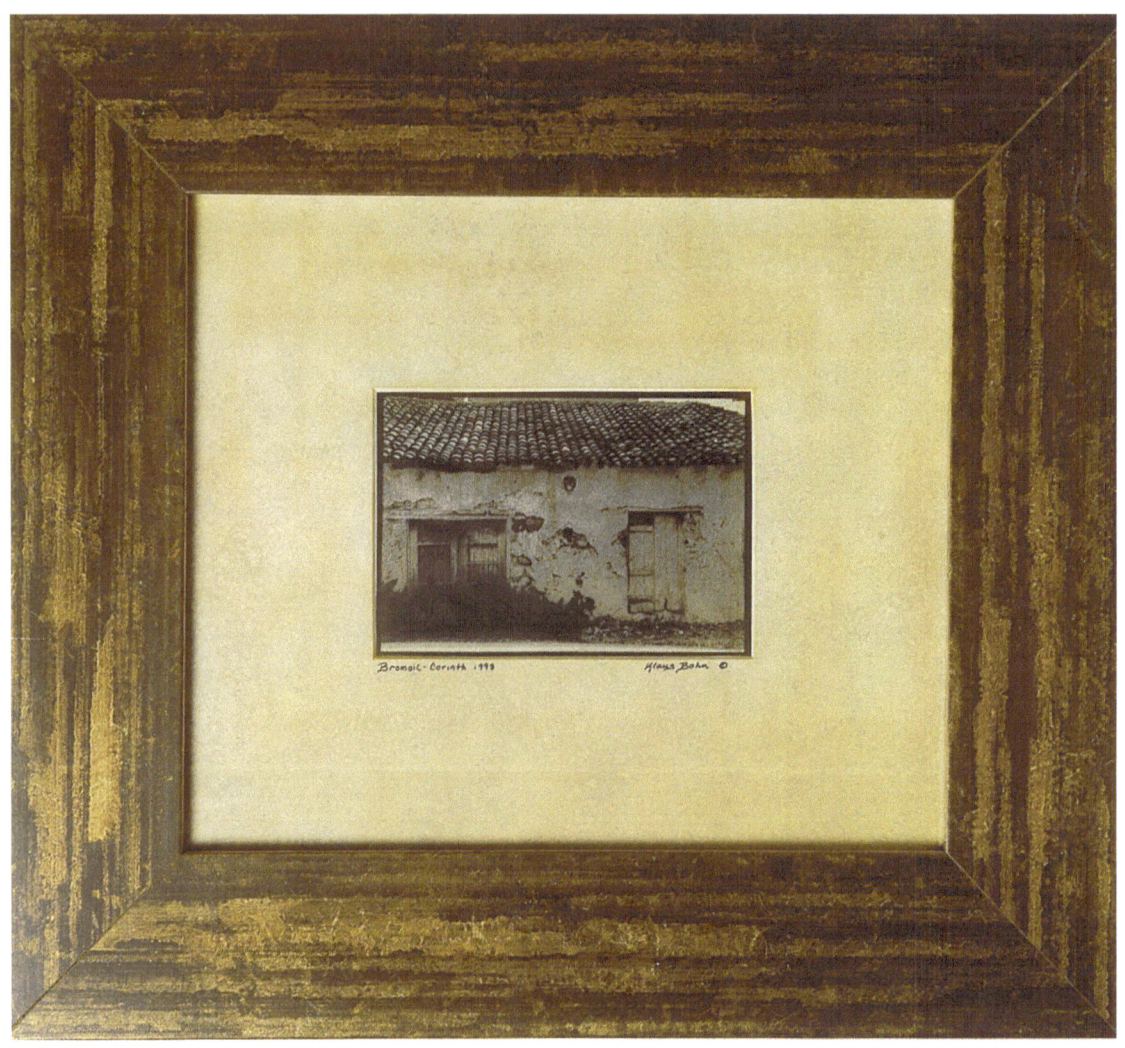

Corinth

We read about the Corinthian people in Paul's writing in the Bible. When I came across this very old house it gave me chills to think that it has so far withstood the test of time. I'm sure the repairs over the years were extensive, and yet the value to keep it up was there for some people to work at it. In a new country like Canada almost everything is new and if it is old, tear it down and build new seems to be our philosophy. Until recently we too have taken up the banner to preserve the past, the history, for up and coming generations.

I guess I liked the windows and door. It felt boarded up to keep out intruders, to leave its history to itself. What took place within over its lifetime we can only imagine, we even fail in that, the story is really untold, a secret for all time.

From the roof to the ground we can appreciate its age. People in the so-called old countries value their aged because of their experiences and the stories they can tell, what they witnessed firsthand, the good times and the hardships. I felt that when I made this image and felt it more deeply producing the bromoil.

I like the mat and wood frame used as it somehow seems to capture the flavour of my mind.

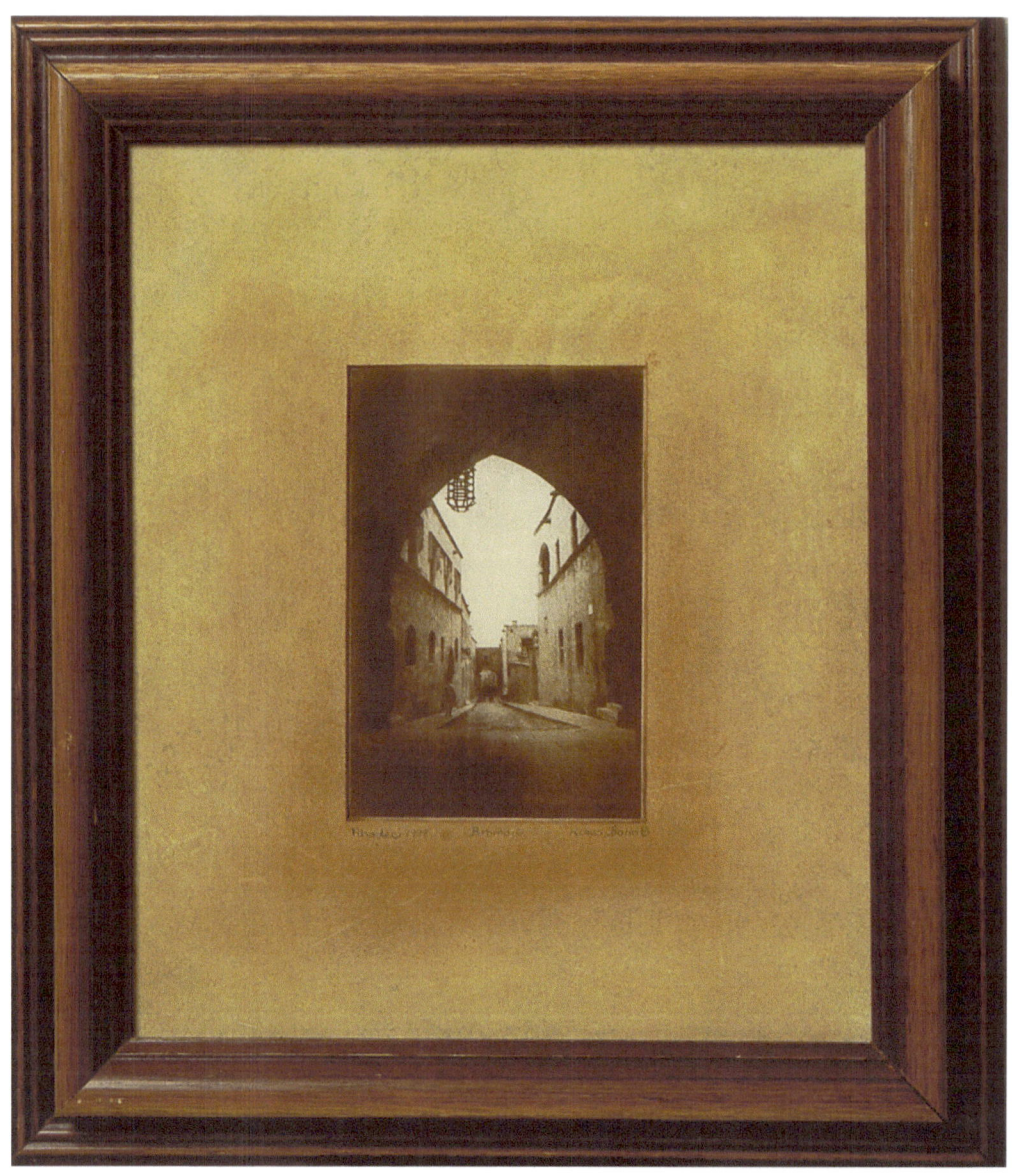

The Arch

Visiting some of the Greek islands has been a joy for me. To engross myself with the history and then walk on those very streets seeing the sights, the mythical caricatures we have read so much about, which were born perhaps of just unbridled imagination.

Rhodes is an island with history and stories that can capture our imagination and hold it ransom for all times. To enter through the arch is like going through history and never coming back the same way as you entered. The distant pathway invites us to come in, beckons us, lures and tempts. There are shadows, like figures almost invisible or ghost like, faint blurry outlines. Isn't that imagination gone wild? To dream the dream of being one of those mythical beings more than Samson, more like mythical dreams of Apollonios Rhodios and of course Hercules.

Before I entered I needed to record the way, the entrance, the only way in. To escape I need to be a bird, part bird part man, a fluke of nature, our DNA mixed up with nature and the heavenly creatures.

Oh I ache with imagination.

How to Contact Klaus Bohn

Should you have any questions regarding this publication or other photography related questions we welcome your inquiries. Please submit your inquiries by visiting Klaus Bohn's **Photographic Art** web site below.

www.photographicartvictoria.com

Index

<u>Notes</u>

Notes

Notes